Artificial Intelligence

Special Issues of Artificial Intelligence: An International Journal

The titles in this series are paperback, readily accessible editions of the Special Volumes of *Artificial Intelligence: An International Journal*, edited by Daniel G. Bobrow and produced by special agreement with Elsevier Science Publishers B.V.

Qualitative Reasoning about Physical Systems, edited by Daniel G. Bobrow, 1985.

Geometric Reasoning, edited by Deepak Kapur and Joseph L. Mundy, 1989.

Machine Learning: Paradigms and Methods, edited by Jaime Carbonell, 1990.

Artificial Intelligence and Learning Environments, edited by W.J. Clancey and E. Soloway, 1990.

Artificial Intelligence
and Learning Environments

edited by
W. J. Clancey and E. Soloway

A Bradford Book
The MIT Press
Cambridge, Massachusetts
London, England

First MIT Press edition, 1990

Reprinted from *Artificial Intelligence: An International Journal*, Volume 42, Number 1, 1990. The MIT Press has exclusive license to sell this English-language book edition throughout the world.

Printed and bound in the Netherlands.

Library of Congress Cataloging-in-Publication Data

Artificial intelligence and learning environments / edited by W. J. Clancey and E. Soloway.
— 1st MIT Press ed.
    p. cm.
    "A Bradford book."
    "Reprinted from Artificial intelligence: an international journal, volume 42, number 1, 1990"
—T.p. verso.
    Includes bibliographical references and index.
    ISBN 0-262-53090-2
    1. Artificial intelligence. 2. System design. 3. Computer-assisted instruction. I. Clancey, William J. II. Soloway, Elliot.
    Q335.A78712 1990
    371.3′34—dc20
                                       90-6333
                                         CIP

Contents

Artificial Intelligence and Learning Environments: Preface

William J. Clancey

Institute for Research on Learning, 2550 Hanover Street, Palo Alto, CA 94304, USA

Elliot Soloway

Department of EECS, University of Michigan, Ann Arbor, MI 48109, USA

The promise of computer-aided instruction (CAI) has always been individualized instruction: providing a learner with an environment that is tailored to his or her learning needs and goals. Although there have been notable successes (e.g., see Larkin et al. [9]), the architecture of CAI systems has been inadequate to provide robust and rich learning environments. Starting in the early 1970s, researchers applied an AI perspective to the problem of creating learning environments. The architecture that evolved during this period suggested that an intelligent CAI system (ICAI) would need: (1) an explicit model of the domain and an expert program that can solve problems in the domain, (2) a model of the student that identifies, at a fine-grained level of detail, what the student understands, and (3) a tutoring model that can provide instruction to remediate misconceptions and/or present new material. Not surprisingly, during this period there was also considerable effort in exploring the psychological questions underlying learning, teaching and understanding. Attempting to summarize and spotlight research in this area, Derek Sleeman and John Seely Brown in 1978 edited a special issue of the *International Journal of Man-Machine Studies* [10]. The title of the book, *Intelligent Tutoring Systems*, gave the field its most commonly used name, ITS.

Rationale for the Collection

Several years ago, we decided that it was again time to assemble a special journal issue that would bring to a general AI audience the advances, insights, and problems of this niche field. ITS research was quite active, with consider-

Artificial Intelligence **42** (1990) 1–6

able financial support from ONR, NSF and other government agencies. Research efforts since the 1970s are particularly interesting because they critically test and improve upon existing AI techniques. For example:

(1) Existing computational models are adapted for use in instructional programs (e.g., Woolf applies discourse analysis in the MENO-TUTOR [13]; Langley et al. [8] apply problem space and discrimination learning to student modeling in ACM).

(2) Explanation and modeling capabilities of existing instructional programs are improved by second-generation knowledge representations (e.g., NEOMYCIN (Clancey and Letsinger [5]), repair theory (VanLehn [12]), STEAMER (Hollan et al. [7]).

However, we found it difficult to gather together a large collection of papers. Excellent work had already been published elsewhere, schedules were over-committed, and publication standards for the journal *Artificial Intelligence* posed relatively narrow and strong constraints.

Research Standards

Our reviewing experience suggested the following characteristics for selecting articles for publication:

(1) The project must make an original and significant contribution to AI, with application to instruction. That is, the research must make a clear statement about the *qualitative modeling of processes* in an instructional setting:
    (a) modeling a *subject matter system* (e.g., a steam-propulsion plant, the neurological system, electronic circuit), *or*
    (b) modeling the *reasoning process* for some task (e.g., diagnosis, control), *or*
    (c) modeling *communication processes* (e.g., Socratic discourse).

(2) The article must make a clear statement of how research goals and assumptions impact on the architecture, and compare other architectures designed for similar goals.

(3) If based on psychological experimentation, the research must at least propose an AI architecture design that the experiments support (regarding the model of the domain, reasoning, or teaching processes, e.g., a knowledge representation and control regime that would explain data about student misconceptions).

(4) If a working program is presented without psychological experimentation, the research must demonstrate generality through multiple problems, domains, and/or student trials.

Overview of the Articles

The articles selected for this special issue are representative of the state-of-the-art:

– John Anderson et al.'s paper provides a crisp characterization of the cognitive theory that informs the design of his tutors in the domains of introductory LISP programming, high-school geometry, and introductory high-school algebra.

– Building on earlier work in plan-based program recognition, Lewis Johnson describes a high-performance system, PROUST, that can identify the nonsyntactic bugs in student-generated programs, for a class of nontrivial introductory programming exercises.

– Drawing on research ranging from qualitative reasoning to cognitive models of learning and teaching, Barbara White and John Frederiksen detail the design of and rationalization for their system, QUEST, which attempts to help students acquire successively more sophisticated qualitative models of basic electric circuits.

Research Trends of the 1980s

We can use these papers as examples to understand how the field has matured in the past decade.

First, the papers demonstrate a wide-ranging exploration of alternatives to tutoring dialogues. Anderson et al. demonstrate that one can build highly detailed and accurate models as students solve a problem, by constraining the possibilities for making mistakes. On the other hand, White and Frederiksen argue that, for physical systems such as electronic circuits, one can build models that are self-evident, revealing for students how circuits work. Students can acquire and debug these models on their own, without the need for a detailed student model or highly tuned tutoring strategies. Finally, Johnson explores a situation where one doesn't have control of the learning environment, and instead accepts whatever the students produce. Students create PASCAL programs using "standard" techniques and submit their 60–100-line programs to PROUST for analysis. The point here is not new to AI—there are no guaranteed approaches, we are still at the stage of investigating domains and contrasting alternative methods.

Second, all three research efforts are directly motivated by psychological concerns. Anderson et al. are absolutely clear on this point: Their goal is to do psychology—developing models of learning and understanding—and their methodology is to implement tutoring systems that allow them to explore their theory. Similarly, White and Frederiksen's interest in qualitative reasoning is not so much to advance that field, per se, but to understand the interplay of qualitative reasoning, human expertise, and instruction. While PROUST is a performance program, not primarily conceived as a cognitive model, Johnson's research was directly motivated by psychological research on the nature of programming expertise.

Third, the research is all strongly driven by empirical trials.

Strikingly, these themes are not dominant in other areas of AI today. A great deal of AI research emphasizes building autonomous agents, rather than viewing AI as just a modeling tool, exemplified by QUEST and PROUST, and implicit in Anderson's de-emphasis of complex teaching dialogues. Second, the questions that AI researchers ask (e.g., concerning the formal properties of a representation and reasoning strategy) need not have psychological relevance. Finally, although empirical trials are important in knowledge engineering and natural language research in general, there is probably no other subarea in which evaluation is so important and yet so difficult as instruction. Here we inherit all the legendary educational problems of evaluating teaching methods and testing what students have learned.

Cognitively oriented, empirical research focusing on AI programming as a modeling methodology can provide insight into a variety of AI problems: Anderson et al.'s claims about the representational and process properties of PUPS (PenUltimate Production System) architecture, White and Frederiksen's perspective on qualitative reasoning, and Johnson's observations on adequacies of various diagnosis strategies, are all pertinent to AI research and deserve attention.

New Perspectives

A number of new perspectives and techniques are shaping the field today (Pea and Soloway [10]):

(a) viewing student modeling as machine learning (and, hence, knowledge acquisition) research;

(b) applying qualitative simulation to modeling complex processes in engineering (e.g., manufacturing process control);

(c) using graphics for explanation;

(d) relating instructional dialogues to natural language discourse research;

(e) determining the extent to which student modeling is possible or necessary;

(f) designing shells for use in multiple domains by teachers;

(g) defining sequences of activities that drive learning by exploration (e.g., through problem-solving failures);

(h) reconceiving epistemological assumptions about the nature of expertise and the differences between novices and experts (Brown, Collins and Duguid [1]);

(i) tackling less formal domains (e.g., history), emphasizing case-based reasoning (Farrell [6]).

Looking towards the future, we believe several shifts in practice need to take place in order for the field to progress:

– More expert systems need to be used for teaching, e.g., there appears to be a preponderance of math, science, and programming applications without balanced concern for engineering, medicine, and social sciences (see [4] for discussion).

– Systems need to be evaluated by applying them in different domains, to determine the generality of the methods and relate them to domain properties. Almost no one studies when programs break and why. Yet, it is precisely failure that helps us understand why programs work, what leverage we are getting from our techniques (see, for example, [3, Chapter 7] or [2, Fig. 6]). Following this advice requires expensive, time-consuming effort, and possibly larger groups working together.

– And most importantly, the small number of knowledgeable AI researchers working on these problems most significantly limits our progress. More support is needed for student researchers. A good goal, albeit controversial, is to provide convincing demonstrations so that engineers, physicians, and other practitioners take for granted that computers are preferable to books for instruction. A secondary goal would be to merge expert systems, natural language, machine learning, knowledge representation, and qualitative simulation in a way that demonstrates synergy in an integrated system.

With focus from a better understanding of the design of practical learning environments and computer power to deliver applications inexpensively, there is good reason to be optimistic that this field will continue to receive the support and research attention that enabled its growth in the past decade.

REFERENCES

1. Brown, J.S., Collins, A. and Duguid, P., Situated cognition and the culture of learning, *Educ. Researcher* **18** (1) (1989) 32–42; also: IRL Rept. IRL88-0008, Institute for Research on Learning, Palo Alto, CA (1988).
2. Clancey, W.J., From Guidon to Neomycin and Heracles in twenty short lessons, ONR Final Report 1979–1985, *AI Mag.* **7** (3) (1986) 40–60.
3. Clancey, W.J., *Knowledge-Based Tutoring* (MIT Press, Cambridge, MA, 1987).
4. Clancey, W.J., Functional principles and situated problem solving, *Behav. Brain Sci.* **10** (3) (1987).
5. Clancey, W.J. and Letsinger, R., NEOMYCIN: Reconfiguring a rule-based expert system for application to teaching, in: W.J. Clancey and E.H. Shortliffe (Eds.), *Readings in Medical Artificial Intelligence: The First Decade* (Addison-Wesley, Reading, MA, 1981) 361–381.
6. Farrell, R., Facilitating self-education by questioning assumptive reasoning, in: *Proceedings AAAI-88*, St. Paul, MN (1988) 2–6.
7. Hollan, J.D., Hutchins, E.L. and Weitzman, L. STEAMER: An interactive inspectable simulation-based training system, *AI Mag.* **5** (2) (1984) 15–27.
8. Langley, P., Ohlsson, S. and Sage, S., A machine learning approach to student modeling, Tech. Rept. CMU-RI-TR-84-7, Robotics Institute, Carnegie-Mellon University, Pittsburgh, PA (1984).

9. Larkin, J. and Chabay, R.R., *Computer Assisted Instruction and Intelligent Tutoring Systems*: *Shared Issues and Complementary Approaches* (Erlbaum, Hillsdale, NJ, 1990).
10. Pea, R. and Soloway, E., Mechanisms for facilitating a vital and dynamic education system: Fundamental roles for education science and technology, Final Report for the Office of Technology Assessment, U.S. Congress (1987).
11. Sleeman, D. and Brown, J.S. (Eds.), *Intelligent Tutoring Systems* (Academic Press, New York, 1982).
12. VanLehn, K., Felicity conditions for human skill acquisition: Validating an AI-based theory, Interim Rept. CIS-21, Cognitive Instructional Science Group, Xerox PARC, Palo Alto, CA (1983); also: Ph.D. Thesis, MIT, Cambridge, MA.
13. Woolf, B. and McDonald, D., Context-dependent transitions in tutoring discourse, in: *Proceedings AAAI-84*, Austin, TX (1984) 355–361.

Cognitive Modeling and Intelligent Tutoring*

John R. Anderson, C. Franklin Boyle,
Albert T. Corbett and Matthew W. Lewis

Advanced Computer Tutoring Project, Carnegie-Mellon
University, Pittsburgh, PA 15213-3890, USA

Introduction

Research on intelligent tutoring serves two goals. The obvious goal is to develop systems for automating education. Private human tutors are very effective [16] and it would be nice to be able to deliver this effectiveness without incurring the high cost of human tutors. However, a second and equally important goal is to explore epistemological issues concerning the nature of the knowledge that is being tutored and how that knowledge can be learned. We take it as an axiom that a tutor will be effective to the extent that it embodies correct decisions on these epistemological issues.

We chose intelligent tutoring as a domain for testing out the ACT* theory of cognition (Anderson [4]). It was a theory that made claims about the organization and acquisition of complex cognitive skills. The only way to adequately test the sufficiency of the theory was to interface it with the acquisition of realistically complex skills by large populations of students. When we read the *Intelligent Tutoring* book, edited by Sleeman and Brown [37], it became apparent that the authors in it were explicitly or implicitly performing such tests of theories of cognition and that it was an appropriate methodology for testing the ACT* theory.

The ACT* theory has been used to construct *performance models* of how students actually execute the skills that are to be tutored and *learning models* of how these skills are acquired. These two cognitive models are incorporated into our tutors and are used to interpret the student's behavior. A performance model consists of a set of correct and incorrect rules for performing the skill in question and is used in a paradigm we call model tracing. In this paradigm we

* This paper reports research supported by a number of grants: NSF Nos. MDR-8470337 and IST-8318629. ONR No. N00014-84-K-0064, and ARI No. MDA 903-85-K-0343.

Artificial Intelligence **42** (1990) 7–49

compare the student's responses to the rules in the model in an attempt to follow in real time the cognitive states that the student goes through in solving a problem. The learning model consists of a set of assumptions about how the student's knowledge state changes after each step in solving a problem. This model is employed in knowledge tracing (as opposed to model tracing) to track the changes in the student's knowledge across problems. The information that results from knowledge tracing can be used to disambiguate alternative interpretations in model tracing and can be used for selecting problems to optimize learning.

We are currently working on tutors for beginning LISP programming [35], for proof generation in high-school geometry [8], and for solving algebraic manipulation and word problems [30]. These domains were selected because they involve the acquisition of well-defined skills and we can catch students at the point where they are just beginning to learn the skill. Our LISP tutor currently teaches a successful university-level course, our geometry tutor has completed two years of successful use in a local public high school, and the algebra tutor is being used in a local public high school in the 1987–1988 academic year. We believe that these tutors owe their success to the cognitive principles from which they were derived. However, it is not the case that the cognitive principles have remained unchanged in the face of these applications. In fact, we have found reasons to reject certain assumptions of the ACT* cognitive architecture and are working with a new architecture called PUPS (for PenUltimate Production System). So, even at this early stage of our endeavor, we have seen a fairly profitable flow of influence back and forth between the theory and the application.

This paper has three major sections. Section 1 describes the cognitive theory that serves as the basis for our tutoring endeavors. Section 2 describes the model-tracing methodology and how it derives from our cognitive theory. Section 3 discusses the issues that arise in implementing the model-tracing methodology.

1. The Cognitive Theory

In describing this cognitive theory, we want to make clear from the outset that we are not necessarily describing what is in our tutors. Instead, we are describing a theory that forms the basis for the tutors. If the mind functions according to our theory, then the tutors should prove to optimize the learning process. To derive predictions from our cognitive theory, we have developed a number of simulations of aspects of it. At some points the code in these simulations has been taken over whole cloth for the tutors, at other points it has influenced tutor code, and at other points the tutor code is just a derivation of the theory. Later we will discuss the tutor implementations. We will just outline the basic cognitive theory here. For details and empirical evidence the reader is referred to Anderson [4, 5] and Anderson and Thompson [13].

In both the PUPS theory and its ACT* predecessor, a fundamental theoretical distinction was made between declarative and procedural knowledge. This distinction borrowed its label from the distinction drawn in AI a decade ago (e.g., Winograd [38]) but has been fundamentally transformed to be a psychological distinction. Declarative knowledge is distinguished by the fact that the human system can encode it quickly and without commitment to how it will be used. Declarative knowledge is what is deposited in human memory when someone is told something, as in instruction or reading a text. Procedural knowledge on the other hand can only be acquired through the use of the declarative knowledge, often after trial and error practice, and is further characterized by the fact that it embodies the knowledge in a highly efficient and use-specific way. In the theory, procedural knowledge derives as a by-product of the interpretative use of declarative knowledge. We use the term knowledge compilation to refer to the learning process which creates the procedural knowledge.

1.1. Procedural knowledge: Productions

In the ACT* and PUPS theories, procedural knowledge is represented by a set of production rules that define the skill. Our goal in tutoring is basically to create experiences that will cause students to acquire the production rules which would be possessed by the competent problem solver. It would be worthwhile to examine some examples of productions that are used in our three domains of tutoring—i.e., LISP, geometry, and algebra.

1.1.1. LISP

Below are "Englishified" versions of a couple of the productions that are used in the LISP tutor:

> IF   the goal is to merge the elements of lis1 and lis2 into a list,
> THEN use append and set as subgoals to code lis1 and lis2.

> IF   the goal is to code a function on a list structure and that function must inspect every atom of the list structure and the list structure can be arbitrarily complex,
> THEN try car-cdr recursion and set as subgoals
> (1) to figure out the recursive relation for car-cdr recursion
> (2) to figure out the terminating cases when the argument is nil or an atom.

The first is a production that recognizes the relevance of a basic LISP function and the second is one that recognizes the applicability of a recursive programming technique. These and approximately 500 more production rules model an ideal student writing basic LISP code to solve problems that would appear in an introductory LISP textbook. These productions all have this goal decomposition character of starting with some programming goal and decomposing it into subgoals until goals are reached which can be achieved with direct code. For an extensive discussion of a model of beginning LISP programming see [10].

1.1.2. *Geometry*

The character of the production rules underlying the geometry tutor are somewhat different. Below are two examples from the approximately 300 in that system:

> IF   the goal is to prove $\triangle XYZ \cong \triangle UYW$
> and X, Y, W are collinear,
> and U, Y, Z are collinear,
> THEN conclude $\angle XYZ \cong \angle UYW$ because of vertical angles.

> IF   the goal is to prove $\triangle XYZ \cong \triangle UVW$
> and $\overline{XY} \cong \overline{UV}$
> and $\overline{YZ} \cong \overline{VW}$,
> THEN set a subgoal to prove $\angle XYZ \cong \angle UVW$ so SAS can be used.

The first production makes a forward inference from what is known about a problem while the second makes a backward inference from what is to be proved. A proof is completed when a set of subgoals from the to-be-proven statement makes contact with a set of forward inferences from the givens of the problem. The production rules for forward and backward inference are contextually constrained. That is, they make reference not only to the information necessary for application of the rule but also to other information about the proof which is predictive of the aptness of that inference. Thus, for instance, the first rule not only makes reference to the collinearity information which is logically necessary for application of the vertical angle rule, it also makes reference to the fact that these angles are corresponding parts of to-be-proven congruent triangles. For more discussion of the nature of the ideal student model in geometry read [1, 8].

1.1.3. *Algebra*

The production system for the algebra tutor is again somewhat different in character from the production systems for LISP or geometry. Below are seven of the production rules involved in modeling the ideal student's knowledge of distribution:

> IF   the goal is to solve an equation with a subexpression of the form "coefficient(exp1 + exp2)",
> THEN set as a subgoal to rewrite the equation with the subexpression distributed.

> IF   the goal is to rewrite an equation with a subexpression distributed,

THEN set as subgoals
    (1) find the coefficient associated with the subexpression,
    (2) multiply the parenthesized part by the coefficient,
    (3) replace the subexpression by the product.

IF   the goal is to find the coefficient of "term",
THEN the answer is 1.

IF   the goal is to find the coefficient of "− term",
THEN the answer is −1.

IF   the goal is to find the coefficient of "num term",
THEN the answer is num.

IF   the goal is to multiply "num1" by "term1 + term2",
THEN set as subgoals
    (1) to multiply term1 by num1,
    (2) to multiply term2 by num1,
    (3) to combine the two products.

IF   the goal is to multiply an expression by a number,
THEN set as subgoals
    (1) to find the coefficient associated with the expression,
    (2) to multiply the coefficient by the number,
    (3) to combine the product with the rest of the expression.

These rules would be invoked if, for instance, there were an expression of the form ... $3(5x + 2)$ ... somewhere in the equation to be solved. The first rule recognizes the applicability of distribution and the second sets three subgoals to accomplish this. The third and fourth rules are special cases of extracting coefficients of 1. The fifth applies in this case and extracts the coefficient of 3. The sixth rule decomposes the distribution into two simpler multiplications. The final production sets the subgoals to extract the 5 from the $5x$, multiply 5 by 3, and then to combine the 15 with x.

The algebra rules highlight the issue of grain size which is also an issue for other production systems. We could have compacted all of these rules into a single production rule which recognized and applied distribution to the equation in one fell swoop (as, for instance, Sleeman [36] does). On the other hand, we could have broken each of these steps into multiple substeps. For instance, note that we do not decompose the process of calculating the product of num1 and num3 into a set of substeps as it might well be implemented cognitively. Our decision about the level at which to model the student was determined by pedagogical considerations. Students entering the algebra course usually have their multiplication skills well-learned and do not need to be tutored on these. In contrast, students do have problems with the subcomponents of distribution and so we need to separate these out for purposes of separate tutoring.

An implication is that the production rules that we use in the algebra tutor, and indeed in the other tutors, represent only upper levels of the skill. These productions set subgoals which are met by other productions whose action we do not bother to simulate. These include such things as the actual typing of answers into the computer. The assumption is that such productions, below the level that we are modeling, are well-learned.

While the production systems for the different domains do have some features in common, the production rules in each domain create different goal structures. Our learning theory would predict that the different task structures of the different domains produce different organizations of the production rules. Generating LISP code is a design activity and lends itself to a problem decomposition structure. The search character of generating geometry proofs produces an opportunistic structure in which there can be large switches of attention among parts of the proof. The linear structure of the algebra equations and the algorithmic character of algebra equation solving produces the symbol substitution character of the algebraic rules. One of the major functions of a tutor for a particular domain should be to communicate the ideal problem-solving structure of that domain.

1.2. Declarative knowledge: PUPS structures

According to our cognitive theory, knowledge is initially encoded declaratively in what we have come to call PUPS structures. At first these structures are used by weak problem-solving productions. As a result of this activity, the knowledge is converted into use-specific production form. PUPS structures are basically schema-like structures which are distinguished by the fact that they have certain special slots which prove critical to their interpretive application in problem solving. These include the function slot which serves to indicate the function of the entity represented by the structure, the form slot which indicates its form or physical appearance, and the precondition slot which states any preconditions that must be satisfied for that form to achieve that function. To illustrate such structures let us consider how an ideal student might encode the following fragment of text from the second edition of Winston and Horn [39, p. 24]:

The value returned by car is the first element of the list given as its argument.

```
(CAR '(FAST COMPUTERS ARE NICE))
   FAST
```

This Winston and Horn example is interesting because it contains a nice juxtaposition of some abstract instruction with a specific example. However, the PUPS encodings of the two (given below) are basically structurally isomorphic. The abstract encoding of **car** indicates in its function slot that it serves as the function in the abstract LISP code represented by **car-structure**. The representation of **car-structure** shows in its form slot the abstract template for function calls involving **car** and in its function slot it specifies what these function calls calculate. The **example1** structure has the same form as **car-structure**, except that an argument is specified. The other PUPS structures encode that argument and the value returned by the example call.

car
ISA: function
FUNCTION: (function-in **car-structure**)
FORM: (text **car**)

car-structure
ISA: lisp-code
FUNCTION: (calculate-first **arg**)
FORM: (list **car arg**)

example1
ISA: lisp-code
FUNCTION: (illustrate **car**)
                (calculate-first **lis**)
FORM: (list **car lis**)

lis
ISA: list
FUNCTION: (argument-in **example1**)
                (hold (**fast computers are nice**))
FORM: (text '(**fast computers are nice**))

fast
ISA: atom
FUNCTION: (value-of **example**)
                (first **lis**)
FORM: (text **fast**)

The structures above represent the outcome of successful encoding of the text; however, it should be stressed that there is a lot of room for "misunderstanding" (incorrect encoding). Clearly, a critical issue for learning is correct interpretation of the instruction. One problem with virtually all instructional material is that it omits many things that the student needs to know in order to perform the tasks, and the student is left to figure them out by trial and error experimentation. One of the payoffs in developing an ideal student model, even before it is used in tutoring, is that it provides a cognitive analysis of what the student really needs to know. Instruction can then be designed to communicate that. In our work we have found that instructional materials designed to communicate all the information in the ideal model (and to not waste prose communicating non-information) are more effective than standard texts even without a tutor. This emphasis on economy and focus in instruction has been confirmed by a number of other researchers (Carroll [20], Reder, Charney and Morgan [34]). It is the motivation for our text on LISP (Anderson, Corbett and Reiser [9]).

However, we believe that it is not possible to avoid all or even most misinterpretations. In communicating unfamiliar material there is the inevit- able difficulty of the student being weak on the key concepts. For instance, we have never observed a student go from reading any textbook on LISP to practicing that knowledge without errors. One important role for a tutor is to monitor for these errors of misunderstanding and correct them as they show up in the performance of a task.

1.2.1. *Interpretive use of declarative knowledge*

We assume that the declarative PUPS structures illustrated above are deposited in memory essentially as the product of language comprehension. It is im- portant that the necessary structures get encoded correctly, but this is by no means the end state of the learning process. These structures do not directly lead to any performance and it is necessary to interpret them to get perfor- mance. This interpretive process is of high demand cognitively and is a major cause of slips in performance [11, 32]. Thus, it is important to create produc- tions like the ones in the ideal model which will automatically apply the knowledge.

There is essentially a double loop of inefficiency promoted by interpretive use of declarative knowledge. The outer loop involves a search through the operations the student knows to find an appropriate next step. For instance, a student might search through all the postulates for proving the triangles congruent: side-side-side, side-angle-side, etc. While it is not possible to entirely avoid search, the productions in the ideal model have features built into them that greatly cut down on this search. The example productions we displayed earlier illustrate this in that they include heuristic tests that check the likelihood that a rule of inference would contribute to a final proof. The inner loop involves the analogical application of a declarative PUPS-structure repre- sentation of an operation to the problem at hand in order to produce a response. This analogical application of declarative knowledge is costly in terms of the amount of information that must be held in working memory. For instance, a great deal of prolonged effort can go into an attempt to map the general statement of the side-angle-side postulate to a specific problem [2]. Once the corresponding information is proceduralized, however, its application makes a much smaller demand on working memory.

1.2.2. *Analogy*

We have observed that the major way that students solve problems involving concepts is by analogy to examples of solutions involving these concepts. To illustrate the analogy process, suppose the student has the goal of getting the first element of the list $(A \, B \, C)$. This is represented by the PUPS structures below:

goal1
ISA: lisp-code
FUNCTION: (calculate-first **lis2**)
FORM: ?

lis2
ISA: list
FUNCTION: (hold (**A B C**))
FORM: ?

As is typically the case in the PUPS representation of a problem-solving situation we have PUPS structures with functions represented but forms empty. The goal is to devise a form that satisfies each functional specification. Both of the required forms can be calculated by analogy to the earlier PUPS structures created from comprehension of the Winston and Horn instruction. Using **example1** as the source for the analogy and **goal1** as the target, PUPS creates the following analogy:

function(example1):form(example1)::function(goal1):?

In solving this analogy, **lis** from **example1** is mapped to **lis2** from **goal1** and the specification (LIST **CAR** lis2) is created for the **goal1** form slot. A similar analogy between **lis** and **lis2** leads to the description (LIST '(**A B** C)) for the form slot of **lis2**. This constitutes a solution to the problem.

1.3. Knowledge compilation

What we have just described is a solution by analogy for a specific example problem. Such analogical reasoning is not optimal for problem solving, however, because it is costly to compute the mapping, and because it will only work when there is an example at hand. Therefore, knowledge compilation tries to analyze the essence of the analogical solution and generate a production rule that can produce the solution at will. Basically, it does this by looking at the problem states before and after generating the analogical solution and creating a production rule that maps one onto the other. Essential to knowledge compilation is diagnosing what was critical in the before situation and what is critical in the solution. This depends on the semantics of the PUPS structure. The result of the compilation process for this example is a production with one variable (=list) that can bind to any list:

IF   the goal is to get the first element of =list,
THEN type (car =list).

The knowledge compilation process that produced this has to know about the correspondences computed in calculating the analogy. Thus, this learning mechanism has built into it knowledge of how PUPS structures are interpreted in analogy.

A second thing knowledge compilation will do is eliminate some of the relatively blind search that characterizes early problem solving. Consider the diagram in Fig. 1, which shows a problem that appears early in the geometry problem sequence. The student is given that two sides of the triangles are congruent and must try to prove that the triangles are congruent. At this point the student has only been taught the side-side-side and side-angle-side postulates for proving triangles congruent. One student, not atypical, was observed to (1) try side-angle-side but fail because there is not an angle congruence; (2) try side-side-side but fail because only two sides are given as congruent; (3) apply the definition of congruence to infer that the measure of $\overline{AD}$ is equal to the measure of $\overline{CD}$; (4) apply the reflexive rule to infer $\overline{AD}$ is congruent to itself; and, (5) finally, apply the reflexive rule, to infer that $\overline{BD}$ is congruent to itself. This last step was the key one that allowed the student to apply the side-side-side rule to achieve his goal. It seemed that the subject engaged in an almost random search of legal operators until he came across one that was useful.

Knowledge compilation creates rules that skip over the steps that were not relevant to the final solution and tries to produce a rule that connects key features in the original situation with the ultimately useful operator. The rule that should be produced in this case is:

IF   the goal is to infer $\triangle XYZ \cong \triangle UYZ$,
THEN infer $\overline{YZ} \cong \overline{YZ}$ because of the reflexive property of
        congruence.

Note this rule is not specific to the solution of this problem by side-side-side

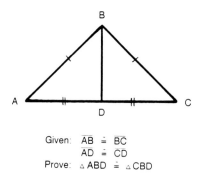

Given: $\overline{AB} \doteq \overline{BC}$
        $\overline{AD} \doteq \overline{CD}$
Prove: $\triangle ABD \doteq \triangle CBD$

Fig. 1. A problem that occurs early in the problem sequence used with the geometry tutor.

nor to the fact that there are already two sides proven congruent. This is what we noted of our subject: He emerged from this episode with a tendency to infer that the shared side of two triangles is congruent to itself whenever he set as his goal to prove these triangles congruent.

This geometry example illustrates the general features of learning from search: If the student applies a number of operators and some of the operators prove successful—in the geometry example a number of inferences were applied and one was part of the final proof—then some knowledge may be proceduralized while additional declarative structures may be formed that encode how the operators achieved their successful function. With subsequent practice these additional declarative structures can lead to the formation of more productions. It is critical that the students properly encode their experience and this is again where tutors can be critical—by assuring the proper encoding of the experience. So, for instance, in the reflexive case discussed above, if the student represented the function of the rule as establishing side-side-side, he would have created too specific a rule. On the other hand, if he represented it as just making a legal inference, he would have created too general a rule.

1.4. Strengthening

In addition to knowledge compilation, there is a simple strengthening of declarative and procedural knowledge with use. As knowledge becomes strengthened it comes to be applied more rapidly and reliably. There is ample empirical evidence for such a simple learning process in humans although its exact nature is in some dispute [2]. The major implication of a strengthening-like process for tutoring concerns the introduction of new knowledge. As the execution of acquired knowledge becomes more proficient there is more capacity left over to properly process the new knowledge.

1.5. Other learning mechanisms?

An important characteristic of this model is what it does not contain. Unlike the ACT* line of learning theories there are no inductive learning mechanisms that automatically compare the current situation with past situations and try to form generalizations and discriminations about when rules will and will not apply. This is not to say that subjects do not engage sometimes in inductive behavior as a conscious problem-solving activity—they certainly do. Rather the claim is that there is not an automatic learning mechanism of the status of compilation and strengthening. Generalizations and discriminations are declarative knowledge structures produced by problem-solving productions rather than productions produced by automatic learning mechanisms. There is a fair amount of evidence that people are aware of their inductive generalizations and discriminations (Lewis and Anderson [29], Dulany, Carlson and Dewey [24]).

This has major implications for instruction. Rather than leaving students to induce generalizations and discriminations from carefully juxtaposed examples, which would have been the pedagogical implication of ACT*, one should simply tell the student what the critical features are. Thus, if a student is overusing the vertical angle inference, he should be told the circumstances under which he wants to use it. This is not to argue that examples are not important, but they should be annotated with information about what they are supposed to illustrate.

2. Converting Theory to Tutoring: Model Tracing

This theory of knowledge acquisition is radical in the juxtaposition of its simplicity and its claim to completeness. To review, learning in the theory involves:

(1) acquisition of new declarative knowledge by the processing of experience through existing productions (e.g. for language comprehension);
(2) application of declarative knowledge to new situations (i.e., situations for which productions do not exist) by means of analogy and pure search;
(3) compilation of domain-specific productions;
(4) strengthening of declarative and procedural knowledge.

Probably there is little controversy that these things (or things very similar to them) are involved in knowledge acquisition, but the issue is whether these assumptions are sufficient to account for all knowledge acquisition. The question is how to put that theory to test. As argued in detail elsewhere [6] our tutoring work is a methodology for testing the theory. Since the design of the tutors is based on the theoretical analysis, the success of the tutors, as measured by post tests and total learning time, is one test of the theory. Moreover, one can ask whether detailed analyses of the student's interaction with the tutor accord with theoretical predictions.

The simplicity of the underlying theory maps onto a rather straightforward tutoring methodology that we call model tracing. The theory provided us with a *performance model* which specifies how a student's knowledge state will map onto performance on a particular problem. The performance model can be used to interpret the student's performance on a particular problem. Instruction is generated to address any confusions that the student is interpreted as showing and to keep students on a correct solution path. In addition, a *learning model* which specifies how the student's knowledge state will change as a result of problem-solving experiences can be used to trace the student's knowledge state over time. Problems and accompanying instruction are selected to practice the student on productions that are diagnosed as weak or missing in the student's knowledge state.[1] Given this structuring of the learning situation, we trust the automatic learning mechanisms in (1)–(4) above to move the student forward on an optimal learning trajectory. In the following sections we will give some examples of this model-tracing methodology. Then, we will discuss some issues in implementing it.

2.1. The LISP tutor

The LISP tutor is based on our earlier efforts to model learning to program in LISP [10]. Appendix A contains a dialogue with a student coding a recursive function to calculate factorial. This does not present the tutor as it really appears. Instead, it shows a "teletype" version of the tutor where the interaction is linearized. In the actual tutor the interaction involves updates to various windows. In the teletype version the tutor's output is given in normal type while the student's input is shown in bold characters. These listings present "snapshots" of the interaction; each time the student produces a response, we have listed his input along with the tutor's response (numbered for convenience). The total code as it appears on the screen is shown, although the student has added only what is different from the previous code (shown in boldface type). For instance, in episode (2) he has added "zero" as an extension of "(defun fact (n) (cond ((".

In the first line, when the subject typed "(defun", the template

$$(\text{defun} \ \langle name \rangle \ \langle parameters \rangle \ \langle body \rangle)$$

appeared. The terms in angle brackets ($\langle \ \rangle$) denote pieces of code the student will supply. The subject then filled in the $\langle name \rangle$ slot and the $\langle parameters \rangle$ slot and had started to fill in the $\langle body \rangle$ slot. Parentheses are automatically balanced and syntax is checked. The motivation here is to remove from the student some of the cognitive load required for checking low-level syntax and to enable the student to focus on higher-level coding problems.

Although the student has some difficulty with the syntax of the conditional tests in episodes (1) and (2), he basically codes the terminating case for the factorial function correctly. Typically, we find students have little difficulty with terminating cases but have great difficulty with recursive cases. Therefore, after episode (3) the tutor interrupts the student to see if the student understands how to write the recursive code. When the student's answer to the first question indicates lack of knowledge, the tutor starts a dialogue to guide the student through a design of the recursive function. Basically, it leads the student to construct a couple of examples of the relationship between fact (n) and fact (n − 1) and then gets the student to identify the general relationship.

---

[1] The actual learning system is not simulated in our tutor—rather we more directly (and much more efficiently) calculate its implications.

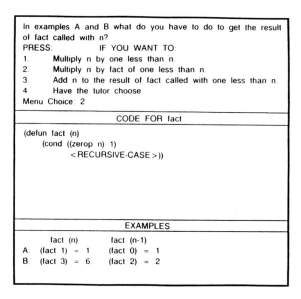

Fig. 2. The screen configuration before episode (4) in Appendix A.

Figure 2 shows the screen image at a critical point in the design of this function.

The dialogue after this point shows two errors that students make in defining recursive functions. The first, in episode (4), is to call the function directly without combining the recursive call with other elements. The second, in episode (5), is to call the function recursively with the same argument rather than a simpler one.

After the student finishes coding the function, he goes to the LISP window and experiments. He is required to trace the function, and the recursive calls embed and then unravel. Figure 3 shows the screen image at this point with the code on top and the trace below it.

This example illustrates a number of features of our tutoring methodology.

(1) The tutor constantly monitors the student's problem solving and provides direction whenever the student wanders off one of the correct solution paths.

(2) The tutor tries to provide help with both the overt parts of the problem solution and the planning. However, to address the planning a mechanism had to be introduced in the interface (in this case menus and short answers) to allow the student to communicate the steps of planning.

(3) The interface tries to eliminate aspects like syntax checking, which are irrelevant to the problem-solving skill being tutored.

```
--- YOU ARE DONE  TYPE NEXT TO GO ON AFTER ---
--- TESTING THE FUNCTIONS YOU HAVE DEFINED  ---

(defun fact (n)
      (cond ((zerop n) 1)
            (t (times n (fact (sub1 n)))))))
```

THE LISP WINDOW

```
= > (trace fact)
(fact)

= > (fact 3)
1 <Enter> fact (3)
|2 <Enter> fact (2)
| 3 <Enter> fact (1)
| |4 <Enter> fact (0)
| |4 <EXIT>  fact  1
| 3 <EXIT>  fact  1
|2 <EXIT>  fact  2
1 <EXIT>  fact  6
6
```

Fig. 3. The screen configuration at the end of the dialogue in Appendix A.

(4) The interface is highly reactive in that it makes some response to every symbol the student enters.

It is interesting to note the contrast between the LISP tutor and the PROUST system of Johnson and Soloway [27]. That system provides feedback only on residual errors in the program and does not try to guide the student in the actual coding. One technical consequence is that the PROUST system has to deal with disentangling multiple bugs. Since the LISP tutor only corrects errors immediately, the code never contains more than one bug at a time.

2.2. The geometry tutor

The geometry tutor is similarly based on our earlier work studying geometry problem solving (Anderson [1–3]). Figure 4 illustrates how a problem is initially presented to a student. At the top of the figure is the statement the student is trying to prove. At the bottom are the givens of the problem. In the upper left corner is a problem diagram. The system prompts the student to select a set of statements using a mouse. Then the system prompts the student to enter a rule of geometric inference that takes these statements as premises. When the student has done so, the system prompts the student to type in the conclusion that follows from the rule. The screen is updated with each step to indicate where the student is. The sequence of premises, rule of inference, and conclusion completes a single step of inference. Figure 5 illustrates the screen

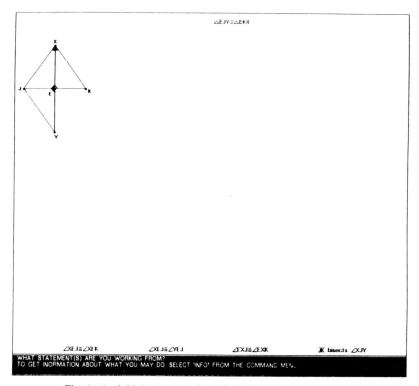

Fig. 4. An initial screen configuration with the geometry tutor.

at the point where the student has selected the definition of bisector to apply to the premise $\overline{JK}$ bisects $\angle XJY$ but has not yet entered the conclusion. A menu has been brought up at the left of the screen to enable the entry of the conclusion. It contains the relations and symbols of geometry. By pointing to symbols in the menu and to points in the diagram, the student can form the new statement $\angle XJK \cong \angle KJY$. We find it useful to have the student actually point to the diagram to make sure the student knows the reference of the abstract statements.

Figure 6 shows the geometry diagram at a still later point. The student has completed the bisector inference and added a plausible transitivity inference, but one that proves not to be part of the final proof. At this point the student begins to flail and has tried a series of illegal applications of rules, the most recent being application of angle-side-angle (ASA) to the premises $\angle EJX \cong \angle EJY$ and $\angle EXJ \cong \angle EXK$. The tutor points out that ASA requires three premises, and so it clearly is inappropriate. Since the student is having so much difficulty, the tutor points the student to the key step in solving this problem: To prove $\triangle EJY \cong \triangle EKX$ one will have to prove $\triangle EJY \cong \triangle EJX$ and

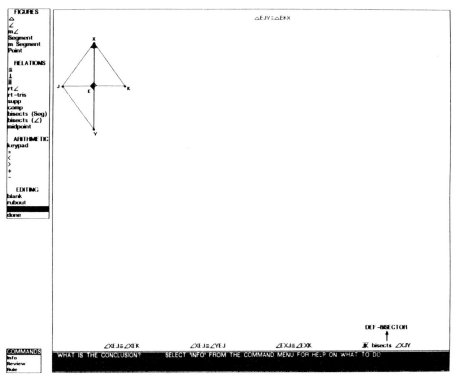

Fig. 5. The screen configuration after the student has selected the premises and the rule and is about to enter the conclusion.

$\triangle EJX \cong \triangle EKX$ and then apply transitivity. The tutor indicates this key step by boxing the conclusion. Thus, the student is asked to use backward inference to enter a rule and a set of premises from which the conclusion logically follows. If necessary, the tutor can step the student through how transitivity of the two triangle congruences will enable the conclusion to be proven. The student then will have the task of proving the two triangle congruences.

Figure 7 shows the state of the diagram at a still later point where the student has proven one of the triangle congruences while the other remains to be proven. It nicely illustrates how students can mix reasoning forward from the givens and reasoning backwards from the conclusions.

Figure 8 shows the completed proof in which there is a graph structure connecting the givens to the to-be-proven statement. Students find such representations of proof solutions enlightening in two ways. First, it enables them to appreciate how inferences combine to yield a proof, something they tend not to get from the traditional two-column formalism. Second, the search inherent in proof generation is explicitly represented. So, for instance, students

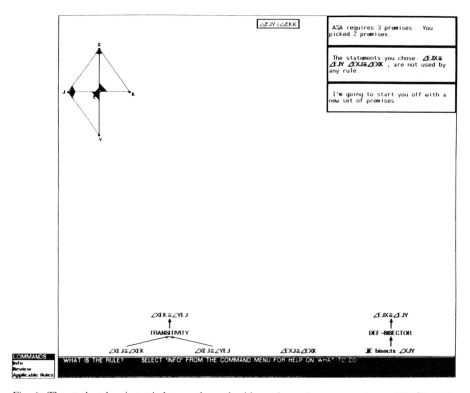

Fig. 6. The student has just tried to apply angle-side-angle to the two premises $\angle EJX \cong \angle EJY$, $\angle EXJ \cong \angle EXK$.

can immediately identify inferences, such as the angle transitivity inference, which are off the main path.

Much of our work on the geometry tutor has been concerned with principles for providing immediate feedback. We will postpone discussion of these principles until the next section on issues involving the model-tracing methodology. The example in Figs. 4–8 illustrates what Brown has referred to as reification. The proof graph makes concrete two abstract features of problem solving in geometry—the logical relationships among the premises and conclusions and the search process by which one hunts for a correct proof. Normally, students have a great deal of difficulty with both of these constructs. By creating an external referent in the form of a proof graph we facilitate instruction about these abstract concepts. Students unanimously report that they prefer this proof graph structure to the more traditional two-column proof form. They typically justify their preferences with the assertion that it is "easier to do a proof" with this formation.

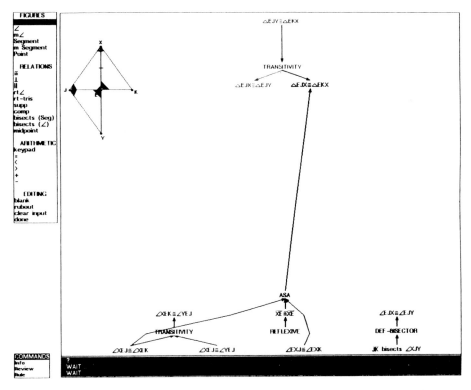

Fig. 7. The student has succeeded in proving one of the two requisite triangle congruences.

2.3. The algebra tutor

The algebra tutor (Lewis, Milson and Anderson [30]) is a more recent endeavor of ours and does not have the prior history of domain study. It reflects an attempt to see how well the methodology that we have developed transfers to a new domain.

So far we have developed a curriculum which takes students through a review of pre-algebra, and through linear and quadratic equations. Figure 9 shows the initial state of the screen at the beginning of solving a linear equation. To the left is a solution window in which the student is going to develop the solution. There are three areas to the right. At the top, there is a blackboard on which the tutor posts messages to the student. In the middle, there is a calculator scratchpad in which the student can perform arbitrary manipulations. At the bottom, there is a menu of choices which the student can point to in order to interact with the tutor. The menu varies; in Fig. 9 it largely consists of options for piecing together a solution to the problem. The student has the option of directly writing in the answer without showing intermediate

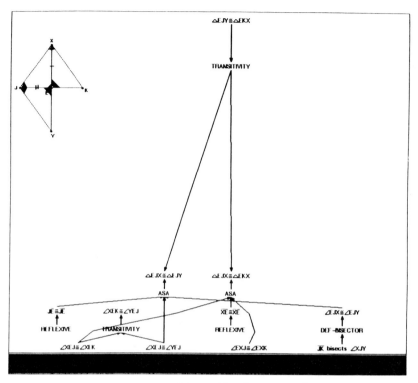

Fig. 8. The proof of the problem is now complete.

results. The student can also decompose the solution into a number of substeps which can be indicated to the tutor by selecting the operations item in the menu.

A new menu replaces the one at the bottom left of Fig. 9 when the student selects "operations". This new menu is shown in Figure 10. The change is that a new menu has come up with possible operations that might be performed on equations. The correct choice at this point would be "cleanup" which refers to eliminating parentheses and collecting like terms. Figure 11 shows the contents of the solution window after the student selects "cleanup." A cleanup form has appeared and the student must figure out what arguments to pass to this operation and what the result will be. The student can point to the equation $3 - 3(x - 4) = -x$ in the solve line above and it will appear as an argument to cleanup. This is one example of many where we try to minimize the number of operations that the student must perform.

Just as the student can decompose "solve-equation" into a number of substeps so the student can decompose "cleanup" into a number of substeps. The first substep for "cleanup" is "distribute." Again, "distribute" can be

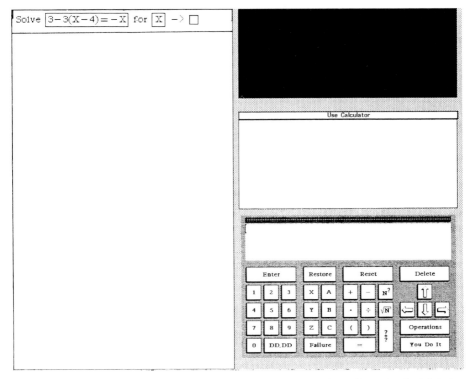

Fig. 9. The algebra tutor's interface as it appears at the beginning of a problem. On the left is the solution window; at the top right is a blackboard for posting messages to the student; at the middle right is a calculator scratchpad where the student can perform primitive operations; and the bottom is a menu of choices for communicating with the tutor.

decomposed into a number of substeps and the first substep is "get-coefficient." Figure 12 shows the screen image with these substeps embedded. Note how the tutor embeds boxes on top of boxes to indicate levels of embedded goals.

Figure 13(a) shows the screen image after the student has completed all of

EQUATIONS	EXPRESSIONS
FRACTIONS	NUMBERS
Add to equation	Cleanup
Collect Constants	Collect Like Terms
Constants Other Side	Distribute
Isolate Solve Var	Multiply Equation
Simplify Equation	Solve
Undo addition	Undo all operations
Undo multiplication	Variables One Side
You Do It	

Fig. 10. The new menu that appears when the student selects the "operations" system in Fig. 9.

Solve $3-3(X-4)=-X$ for X -> ☐

Cleanup ☐ -> ☐

Fig. 11. The solution window after "cleanup" is chosen from Fig. 10.

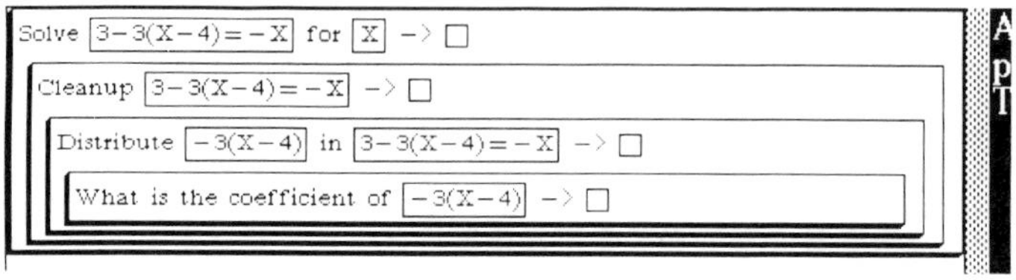

Solve $3-3(X-4)=-X$ for X -> ☐

Cleanup $3-3(X-4)=-X$ -> ☐

Distribute $-3(X-4)$ in $3-3(X-4)=-X$ -> ☐

What is the coefficient of $-3(X-4)$ -> ☐

Fig. 12. A later state of the solution after the student has selected "distribute" as a substep to "cleanup" and "get-coefficient" as a substep to "distribute."

the substeps of cleanup. The screen maintains two levels of completed substeps. Thus, the student can see that cleanup was solved by a "distribute" followed by a "collect." Having finished the cleanup substep the student has turned to the next major step in solving the problem which is to move the variable terms to one side. The student has chosen to try to answer this directly rather than pursue it in substeps. Unfortunately, he has made the classic sign error and entered $15 = -4x$. The tutor recognizes this error and enters a remedial message on the blackboard. This error message is illustrated in Fig. 13(b).

Figure 14 shows the final solution window when the problem is solved. The student finished the move-variables goal and started on the isolate goal.

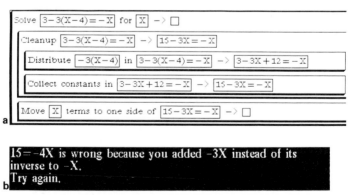

Fig. 13. (a) A later state of the solution window after the student has gone on to try the substep of "move-variable-to-one-side" after completing the "cleanup" step. (b) The error message given to the student who enters $15 = -4x$ as the result for the last step in (a).

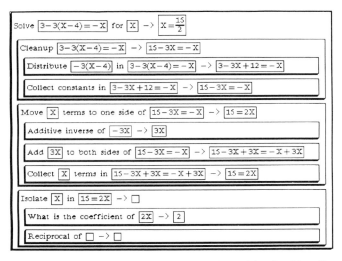

Fig. 14. The final state of the solution window after solving $3 - 3(x - 4) = -x$.

However, in the midst of solving the isolate goal the student saw the answer and chose what is called the popout option. This lets him put in the answer to the isolate goal without filling in the suboperations. Finally the student posted that result as the answer to the top goal of solving the equation.

At all points there is an option on the current menu called "you do it." If the student selects this when an argument or a goal is required, the tutor describes the argument or goal. If the student selects "you do it" when a result is required, the tutor will decompose the task of obtaining the results into a set of substeps unless the result comes from a primitive goal. In this case the tutor just gives the student the result.

As in the case of the other tutors, the algebra tutor moves the student along towards a solution. The one thing unique about the algebra tutor is our policy of decomposing a result calculation into substeps recursively until primitive steps are reached. Our informal observation is that this seems to be pedagogically effective in that it enables the tutor and student to determine the locus of a misconception.

2.4. Summary of the tutors

Underlying each of the tutors is an ideal model of how students should solve the respective problems and a model of how students err. The error model is used to recognize and remediate errors. The ideal model is used to guide students along a correct solution path if necessary. This combined use of the ideal and error model (together called the generic model) is what defines the model-tracing methodology—the tutor traces out the path the student tries to take through the generic model and insists that the student stay on a correct path.

The major activity of the tutor is monitoring students' problem solving. We attempt to create highly interactive interfaces that quickly let the students know when their solutions deviate from ideal solution behavior and just where they deviate. This kind of instructional environment has a highly procedural flavor and contrasts with the more abstract and declarative instruction in some tutoring efforts (e.g., [22]). This reflects fundamental differences in the nature of the knowledge to be communicated and how that knowledge is communicated. Our current tutors are focused on helping the procedural component of learning although we are currently considering extending them to declarative instruction where we might adopt a methodology more like Collins, Warnock and Passafuime [22].

2.5. Evaluating the model-tracing methodology

A critical issue is whether the model-tracing methodology really works in improving the learning of the subject domains. A general problem with work in intelligent tutoring is that it has tended to progress without any empirical feedback as to whether the proposed mechanisms work. What feedback there is has been largely anecdotal. We have been able to perform some systematic tests of the effectiveness of our tutors which we will briefly report here. After reviewing these evaluations we will discuss issues concerned with why such summative evaluations are not completely satisfying and we will try to identify further research directions.

2.5.1. *LISP*

The LISP tutor was systematically evaluated in a course we taught in the fall of 1984. A class of 20 students was divided into two groups counterbalanced according to statistics such as math SATs and prior computing experience. All students attended the same lectures and did the same problems as homework. One group of students did these problems with the LISP tutor and the other group did them in the standard FRANZLISP environment. There was a proctor available to all students to answer questions. The proctor spent most of his time with students who lacked the tutor. We estimate that perhaps 5% of these students' time was spent with the proctor. Thus, we have a fairly controlled comparison of a group of students working with the tutor and a group of students learning in a fairly representative college environment with perhaps a little more access to human help than is typical.

The LISP curriculum taught by the tutor at that time was a subset of the curriculum currently taught. It involved the following nine lessons: an introduction to basic LISP functions, defining new functions, conditionals and predicates, structured programming, input-output, integer-based iteration, integer-based recursion, list-based recursion, and advanced recursion. Figure 15

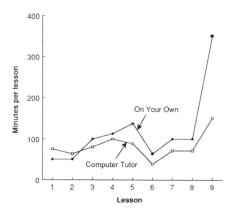

Fig. 15. Comparison of time spent per lesson by subjects learning LISP in the tutor and control groups.

shows the amount of time spent solving the problems in each lesson with and without the tutor. As can be seen, there is very little difference between the conditions over the first four lessons. In fact, students take less time without the tutor on the first two lessons. One reason tutored subjects might spend more time is that the tutor was somewhat slow—a condition that has been improved upon in succeeding years. On the other hand, students are taking more than twice as long without the tutor on the ninth lesson which involves programming some difficult recursive functions. The basic result seems to be that the tutor reduces time on tasks where there is considerable difficulty and search in finding a correct solution. Certainly, subjects in the on-your-own condition spent a lot of time on lesson 9 trying solutions that they had to completely abandon.

Students in the class took two paper-and-pencil exams which provide an assessment of performance outside the learning environment. There was no difference between the two groups on an exam after lesson 6, but a statistically significant advantage for the tutored group appeared following the ninth lesson. Tutored students scored 43% higher on the final exam. All students were required to do a final project without the tutor which involved writing a program to solve the waterjug problem. Tutored students received 10% higher grades, but this did not approach statistical significance.

2.5.2. *Geometry*

The geometry tutor has been used for two years in a local high school. This first year (1985–1986) was devoted primarily to observing its reliability in a classroom setting. The tutor was used throughout the third quarter of the academic year by four classes. Two of these classes consisted of students who were in the regular academic track, one class consisted of students placed in the "scholars" track on the basis of their high level of performance in past math courses, and one class of students consisted of students designated "gifted" on the basis of IQ scores. The results of this evaluation were very encouraging. Students were enthusiastic about using the tutor and all three groups of students showed statistically significant improvement in test scores between a pre-test and a post-test on geometry proofs. The mean score of the students in the regular academic track rose from 44 points on the pre-test to 54 points on the post-test (out of a maximum score of 80 on each test). The mean for the "scholars" track rose from 57 to 63 and the mean for the "gifted" class rose from 55 to 72 points. About 10 points on this scale corresponded to a letter grade difference, so average performance increased a minimum of about a half-grade difference, to as much as a grade and a half across the three groups, although the differences in degree of improvement across classes is not significant.

Thus, the initial use of the tutor proved successful, but what is lacking in this evaluation is an appropriate measure of how well comparable groups of students would have done without the tutor. So, a controlled comparison of tutor and non-tutor classes was carried out in the second year. In this comparison, the same teacher taught five classes which varied in student ability level and whether the tutor was present or not. We also had the teacher instruct one class of larger size in which two students worked with each tutor. In comparisons of classes of similar size and ability, tutored students scored 64 points (out of 80) on the post-test while non-tutored students scored 48 points. This difference was statistically significant.

We ran a regression analysis of the difference among students on the post-test using as predictor variables IQ, grade in the prior year's algebra class, whether the student used the tutor, and finally, if the tutor was used, whether there was a 2–1 ratio of students to tutors. There were significant effects of algebra grade, tutor and student–tutor ratio. Students scored an average of 7 points higher on the post-test with each higher algebra grade, 14 points higher if they used the tutor, but 10 points lower if they were in a 2–1 ratio of students to tutors. This indicates that the tutor has the same predictive impact as a two-letter grade difference in algebra. It also indicates that the tailoring of instruction for a particular student is important.

2.5.3. *Algebra*

Our evaluation of the algebra tutor is more preliminary since we have been using it in laboratory situations only and have not introduced it in the classroom. So far we only have evidence that it produces learning. That is to say, all students who work with it know more about algebra than before they started. We have no evidence that it is better than comparable time spent without the tutor. We hope to address this question in a classroom test in the 1987–1988 school year.

It is a fair summary of this evaluation research to say that our tutors do help. This is a far from obvious outcome. When we started out it was a radical proposal to assert that we could get students to improve their performance by forcing them to follow the steps of our cognitive models. Clearly, if our cognitive models did not have some substantial truth to them, we would have failed miserably. Thus, this positive evaluation outcome is general support for our theoretical position.

Nonetheless, it is hardly satisfactory evidence. We do not really know what features of our tutors produced these positive outcomes nor do we know how optimal our tutors are. The LISP and geometry tutors produce an improvement of about one standard deviation in classroom performance, whereas human tutors are known to produce an improvement of two standard deviations [16]. It is unclear whether performance of human tutors is achievable by computer tutors. Some of the benefit of human tutors might be due to affective reactions to human interaction. In addition, some of the benefits may depend on an ability to process natural language questions and answers that exceed the level that is practically obtainable in computer tutors. On the other hand, there is no reason to believe that human-tutor performance defines an upper bound since humans almost certainly are not always optimal in their decisions. The basic point is that we need to begin to do systematic studies of design variations on our tutors to determine which features of the tutor are critical to our positive results, which are neutral, and which may be preventing us from achieving even more positive results. Such research would also be more illuminating with respect to the underlying theoretical issues. We are just embarking on such a program of research.

3. Implementing the Model-Tracing Methodology

A major prerequisite to implementing a model-tracing tutor is to create all the production rules that will be involved in the tracing. A significant subtask here is adding an adequate set of buggy rules to the student model in order to be able to account for the errors we see. In our experience the best we have been able to do is to account for about 80% of the errors—the remaining being just too infrequent and too removed from the correct answer to yield to any analysis. One approach to coding the systematic errors has been simply to observe the errors students make with our tutor, try to understand their origin, and code the inferred buggy productions one by one into the system. In more recent work such as in our algebra tutor we are trying to generate these errors on a principled basis in a fashion similar to the notable work on subtraction [17, 19] and on algebra [31]. For instance, a frequent source of errors in algebra is forgetting to perform a necessary substep in the calculation.

Given a production set which can model the range of behaviors we see in our students, our tutor design then can be decomposed into three largely independent modules. There is the student module which can trace the student's behavior through its nondeterministic set of production rules. There is the pedagogical module which embodies the rules for interacting with the student, for problem selection, and for updating the student model. The separation between student module and pedagogical module is similar to the separation of instruction from the expert system in a number of tutoring systems, including those of Brown, Burton, and de Kleer [18] and Clancey [21]. Finally, there is the interface which has the responsibility of interacting with the student. As a software engineering issue, these three components can be developed separately with the pedagogical module taking responsibility for controlling the interaction among the three modules—getting interpretations and predictions from the student module and making requests to the interface to present information to the student or to get information from the student. While each module is complex, dividing a major software project into three independent components is a big step in the direction of tractability. Much of the subsequent discussion will be organized around issues involving each of the components.

3.1. The student module

The basic responsibility of the student module is to deliver to the pedagogical module an interpretation of a piece of behavior in terms of the various sequences of production rules that might have produced that piece of behavior. The obvious methodology for doing this is to run our nondeterministic student model forward and see what paths produce matching behavior. While there are complexities and efficiencies that have been added to this basic insight this is the core idea. The rest of the discussion of the student model is concerned with issues raised in trying to implement this core idea.

3.1.1. Nondeterminacy

Nondeterminacy in the production sequence is a major source of problems in implementing the model-tracing methodology. We face nondeterminacy whenever multiple productions in the student module produce the same output. (For instance, in the algebra tutor the student says he wants to apply distribution, and there are multiple possible distributions in the equation.) A special case of this is when productions produce no overt output as when a student is doing some mental calculating or planning. What to do in the case of such planning nondeterminacy is an interesting question. The set of potential paths can explode exponentially as the simulation goes through unseen steps of cognition. Also, the potential for actually effectively tutoring these steps is weakened the greater the distance between the mental mistake and the feedback on that decision. Therefore, one is naturally tempted to query the student as to what he is thinking—that is, to force an association of some output with the mental steps. On the other hand, it is difficult to design an interface which can trace planning in a way that does not put an undue burden on the student. Students often resent even giving vocalized answers to the question "what are you thinking about" and there is reason to believe such simultaneous report generation may interfere with the problem solving [25]. The sample LISP tutor interaction that we traced earlier, in which the student and tutor work through a recursive plan for factorial is one instance of our effort at plan tracing. While we have some evidence that such interactions help, students report that they do not like being slowed down by having to go through such interactions.

Another example of the problem created by nondeterminacy is that misunderstandings and slips can often produce the identical behavior. For instance, students can confuse CONS and LIST in programming either because they really do not understand the difference or as a result of a momentary lapse [11]. The student model must be capable of delivering both interpretations to the tutor, leaving to the tutor the task of assessing the relative probability of the two interpretations and deciding what remedial action should be taken.

3.1.2. *Production system efficiency*

A major complication we face when we try to trace a student's problem solving is that running a production system in real time can create serious problems. Students will not sit still as a system muddles for minutes trying to figure out what the student is doing. They will not pace their problem solving to assist the diagnosis program. Interestingly, our observation has been that human tutors have problems with real-time diagnosis and one of the dimensions on which human tutors become better with experience is real-time diagnosis.

Production systems, for all their advantages, are by and large not the fastest way to solve problems. The inherent computational problems of production systems are exacerbated in tutoring for a number of reasons:

(1) The grain size of modeling is often smaller than would be necessary in expert system applications, and the complexity of the production patterns required to expose the source of student confusions is often considerable.

(2) The system has to consider enough productions at any point to be able to recognize all next steps that a student might produce. This contrasts with many applications where it is sufficient to find a production that will generate a single next step.

(3) Often it is not clear which of a number of solution paths a student is on and the production system has to be used nondeterministically to enable a number of paths to be traced until disambiguating information is encountered.

The production systems we have produced have all involved variations on the RETE algorithm developed by Forgy [26] for pattern matching which has supported many of the OPS line of production systems. However, we have not had good success with simply using OPS as our expert system because the pattern matching for each domain has special constraints upon which we have had to try to optimize. Anderson, Boyle and Yost [8] discuss this issue for the domain of geometry.

A major issue in designing the pattern matcher for a domain is to decide how much detail of the actual problem should be represented. For instance, if one is developing an algebra tutor it is useful to have different representations for the following two expressions during the early stages of teaching factoring:

$$2AB + 4A ,$$
$$2BA + 4A .$$

There is evidence that the first expression can be more easily factored into $2A(B + 2)$ than can the second expression: Commutativity of multiplication is not automatic in many students, and the common factor of $2A$ might not be seen in the second expression above. On the other hand, when we look at students who have mastered algebra and are learning calculus, it is no longer necessary to represent the distinction between these two forms. This means that in calculus we can use certain "canonicalizations" that simplify the pattern matching and reduce the number of productions.

The computational cost associated with implementing such production systems has a space as well as a time dimension. The number of productions can be on the order of thousands to tutor a domain and the RETE algorithm can be space expensive storing partial products of pattern matching.

Of course, it is an open question just how efficient in time and space we can make our production system implementations. In their current form they are just within the threshold of acceptability, which is to say students are barely satisfied with the performance of a machine like a Dandetiger with over three megabytes of memory. However, there are reasons for us not to be satisfied with this performance. In the first place such machines are still a good deal beyond the range of economic feasibility. Secondly, efficiency issues impact on the range of topics we handle. This manifests itself in a number of ways:

(1) Problems tend to become more costly as they become larger even if the larger problems involve the same underlying knowledge. This is because production system working memory tends to increase, as does the nondeterminism. Therefore, there is an artificial size limit on the problems we tutor students on.

(2) Progress into more advanced topics is as much limited by dealing with the added computational burden posed by these topics as with adequately understanding and modeling the domain.

(3) The actual tutoring interactions become limited by the need to reduce nondeterminacy. For instance, some of our tutors force a particular interpreta-

tion of the student's behavior on the student, rather than waiting until the student generates enough of the solution to eliminate the ambiguity.

3.2. Compiling the model tracing

If one looks at all possible sequences of productions that can be generated in any of our models, one finds that it defines a problem space of finite cardinality. That cardinality can be quite large, but often simply because we are looking at different permutations of independent or nearly independent steps in a problem solution. This suggests that if we are clever in our representation of the problem space we need not dynamically simulate the student in order to interpret him. Rather, we can generate the problem space beforehand and just use the student's behavior during problem solving to trace through this pre-completed problem space. Given the cost of real-time simulation with a production system, this seems that it might be a worthwhile step. In one case, we obtained a 50% performance improvement in our LISP tutor by a partial implementation of this step. In a major project just completed, we used this technique to transfer the geometry tutor from the Dandetiger to the Macintosh and got a significant improvement in performance.

There are other advantages to having the complete problem space compiled in advance of the actual tutoring session. This makes it easy for the tutor to look ahead and see where a step in the problem solution will lead. Often in a proof tutor, a production rule will be favored by the ideal model but in fact not lead to a solution. For instance, there are geometry problems where even experts make certain inferences which do not end up as part of the final proof. It is the sort of heuristic inference which is successful nine times out of ten but is not useful one time in ten. If the tutor recommended dead-end steps just because the ideal model makes them, the student would quickly loose faith in the tutor. Human tutors also tend to look ahead to make sure that their recommendations lead somewhere.

3.3. The pedagogical module

One interesting observation about our overall tutoring framework is that it is possible to decouple the pedagogical strategy from the domain knowledge.[2] Domain knowledge resides in both the student model and the interface. It is the pedagogical module that relates the two and which controls the interaction. This module does not really require any domain expertise built into it. It is concerned with (1) what productions can apply in the student model, not the internal semantics of the productions; (2) what responses the student generates and whether these responses match what the productions would generate, not

---

[2] This point was demonstrated much earlier in GUIDON (Clancey [21]). Our tutoring rules were much influenced by the Clancey GUIDON rules.

what these responses mean; and (3) what tutorial dialogue templates are attached to the productions, not what these dialogues mean.

We are in fact working on a new PUPS-based tutor [12] which is a limited realization of this idea. It is concerned with tutoring three programming languages—LISP, PASCAL, and PROLOG. We hope to build student models for different programming domains independent of tutoring strategy and to build different tutors to implement variations on tutoring strategy independent of domain. Specific tutors can be generated by crossing the tutorial module with the domain module without tuning one to another.

There are theoretical reasons for believing that we can create domain-free tutoring strategies and that the optimal tutoring strategy will be domain-free. Our theory of human skill acquisition leads us to believe that the basic learning principles are domain-free. The optimal tutoring strategy would simply optimize the functioning of these learning principles.

However, in our current running systems we have built a separate tutor for each domain. While it is not the case that the tutoring strategies they implement are identical, they are quite similar and we have claimed publicly that they are attempts to embody a strategy based on the ACT learning theory [7]. It is useful to identify what the features of the common tutoring strategy are and what the variations on the strategy could be. It will become clear that, when we look at any dimension of tutoring, there are conflicting considerations as to what the optimal choice should be.

3.3.1. *Immediacy of feedback*

The policy on immediacy of feedback is well illustrated by the LISP tutor. The LISP tutor insists that the student stay on a correct path and immediately flags errors. This minimizes problems of indeterminacy. There are a number of reasons for desiring immediacy of feedback besides this technical one. First, there is psychological evidence that feedback on an error is effective to the degree that it is given in close proximity to the error [14, 29]. The basic reason for this is that it is easier for the student to analyze the mental state that led to the error and make appropriate correction. Second, immediate feedback makes learning more efficient because it avoids long episodes in which the student stumbles through incorrect solutions. Third, it tends to avoid the extreme frustration that builds up as the student struggles unsuccessfully in an error state.

However, we have discovered a number of problems with the use of immediate feedback:

(a) The feedback has to be carefully designed to force the student to think. If at all possible, the feedback should be such that the student is forced to calculate the correct answer rather than just being given the answer [14]. It is important to learning that the student go through the thought processes that generate the answer rather than copy the answer from the feedback.

(b) Sometimes students would have noticed the error and corrected it if we just gave them a little more time. Self-correction is preferable when it would happen spontaneously. As we know, people tend to remember better what they generate themselves [4, Chapter 5].

(c) Students can find immediate correction annoying. This is particularly true of more experienced students. Thus, novice programmers generally liked the immediate feedback feature of our LISP tutor whereas experienced programmers did not. While our goal is not to produce positive affective response, it probably does have some impact on learning outcome.

(d) Often it is difficult to explain why a student's choice is wrong at the point at which the error is first manifested because there is not enough context. To consider a simple example, compare a student who is going to generate (append (list x) y) where (cons x y) is better. It is much easier to explain the choice after the complete code has been generated rather than after "(append" has been typed.

There is no reason why the model-tracing paradigm commits us to immediate feedback, although as noted there are psychological reasons for choosing it. One of the variations we would like to explore in the LISP tutor is a system that gives feedback after "complete" expressions like (append (list x) y). This will give the student some opportunity for self-correction and also provide a larger context for instruction. On the other hand the distance between error and feedback will still be limited. For more discussion of the different feedback options in the LISP tutor see [23].

3.3.2. Sensitivity to student history

By and large the only student model we use is our generic model which is a composite of all correct and incorrect moves that a student can make. At each point in time we are prepared to process all the production rules that we have seen any student use, correct or buggy. If students make an error we give the same feedback independent of their history. The only place we show sensitivity to student history is in presenting remedial problems to students who are having difficulties. It is relatively easy to implement a generic student model, and the question is whether there is any reason to go through the complexity of tailoring the model to the student.

There is one aspect of this generic student model which derives from our theory of skill acquisition and another aspect which does not. The aspect that is theoretically justified is the belief that there are not different types of students who will find different aspects of a problem differentially hard. That is, our theory does not expect individual differences or traits in learning, beyond some overall difference in ability or motivation. The theory implies that all people learn in basically the same way. Of course, it is an open question whether there is empirical evidence for the theory on this score. In our own research it does appear that students differ only in a single dimension of how well they learn

[6]. Despite valiant searches we have yet to find evidence that one set of productions cluster together as difficult for one group of students while a different cluster of productions are difficult for another group of students.

The aspect of a generic model that does not derive from the theory is the assumption that past history of use with a rule implies nothing about the interpretation of a current error. We have evidence that different subjects continue to have trouble with specific different rules. (This is to be contrasted with a trait view that says there is a nonsingleton set of productions that a number of subjects will have difficulty with.) If the student has had a past history of success on a rule it is more likely that error reflects a slip, rather than some fundamental misunderstanding. Currently, our tutors treat all errors as if they reflected fundamental misconceptions and offers detailed explanation, but the better response sometimes would be simply to point the error out.

3.3.3. *Problem sequence*

The existing tutors implement a mastery model for controlling the selection of problems to present to the student. They maintain an assessment of the student's performance on various rules and have knowledge of what problems exercise what rules. The tutors will not let the student move on to problems involving new rules until the student is above a threshold of competence on the current rules. If the student has not demonstrated mastery, the tutor will select additional problems from the current set which exercise rules on which the student is weak.

While such a mastery policy for problem sequence may seem reasonable and there is evidence in the educational literature for its effectiveness [16], it is interesting to inquire as to its underlying psychological rationalization. Why not go onto new problems while the student is weak on current knowledge and teach both the new knowledge and the old weak knowledge in the context of the new problems? Fundamentally, the mastery policy rests on a belief in an optimal learning load—that if we overload a student with too many things to learn, he will learn none of them well. On the other hand, students are advanced to new material at some point when further training on the old material could have improved their performance even more. So there is a countervailing assumption about diminishing returns—that at some point the gain in improving performance on old rules is not equal to gain in learning new rules.

Our choice about exactly where to set the mastery level has been entirely ad hoc. In the ACT and PUPS theories working-memory load affects learning and problems pose less load as they become better learned. However, these processes are not specified in a way that enables us to define an optimal next problem. The issue of problem sequence and mastery levels remains to be worked out in a model-tracing paradigm.

3.3.4. *Declarative instruction*

A student's first introduction to the knowledge required to solve a class of problems is typically not from the tutor; rather it is declarative instruction typically provided in a textbook or lecture. How should this declarative instruction be formulated to make it maximally helpful in learning the skill? Given our analysis of learning by analogy, instruction should take the form of examples appropriate for mapping into problem solutions. Given our PUPS structures, it is not enough that the student simply have the form slots of these structures properly represented; it is critical for successful learning that the student have properly represented the function of these structures and any prerequisites to these structures achieving their functions. For example, Pirolli and Anderson [33] showed that, while all students learn recursive programming by analogy to existing programs, what determines how well they learn is how well they represent how these programs achieve their function. Basically, students often understand an example only superficially and thus emerge from analogy with mischaracterizations of the range of problems for which the structures in the example are appropriate.

In our efforts to create textual instruction to go along with our tutors, we have focused on the issue of giving good examples for purposes of mapping and trying to assure that the student achieves the right encoding of the example. Indeed, we have produced a LISP textbook [9] which consists mainly of carefully crafted examples with explanation aimed at promoting the right encoding. However, what is missing is interactive instruction to assure that the students have encoded the example correctly.

3.4. The interface

One might have thought that the discussion to this point would complete the description of our tutoring systems. We have stated how a tutor models a student and how it uses that model to achieve pedagogical goals. However, the discussion is abstract and leaves completely unspecified what the student actually experiences, which is the computer interface. We have learned that design of the interface can make or break the effectiveness of the tutor. Below are just a few examples:

(1) Early in the history of the LISP tutor we had a system in which the student entered code in a buffer and then dispatched the contents of that buffer to appear in a code window. Students get confused with the system because they were frequently working on one goal while the tutor was processing a different goal. We changed this to a system where one typed the new code right into the old code and these confusions disappeared.

(2) An early version of the algebra tutor had a system in which students entered a next equation, the tutor figured out what steps they engaged in, and

tried to give appropriate feedback and point them back to the right track. The problem was that the students' error might well have occurred at some intermediate step that the students were no longer fixated upon (e.g., adding two fractions in the course of moving a number across the equation sign). It was very difficult to communicate to the student what the problem was. We introduced the system described earlier in this paper in which the student actually stepped through the microsteps of the transformation in a relatively painless way with the system. The tutor could flag the errors as they occurred and these miscommunications disappeared.

(3) We used to have our students type in geometry statements through a typical keyboard. Given the rather special syntax of geometry statements, students would often enter basically correct statements in syntactically incorrect form. After entering a syntactically incorrect statement, the system would tell them it could not understand what they meant. This response by the system often caused them to doubt their understanding of the problem. To remedy this we introduced a real-time parser which flagged them as soon as they entered a character which would make their expression syntactically illegal. Again our difficulties disappeared.

(4) The graphical structure we use to represent geometry statements (Figs. 4–8) seems to be the key to enabling students to understand the structure of a proof even though it is essentially isomorphic in logical structure to a linear proof. The graphical structures make explicit the logical relationships students would have to infer.

(5) In all of our tutors it seems critical to spend considerable time fashioning the English to make it as brief and as understandable as possible. If students face great masses of hard-to-understand prose, they will simply not process the message.

(6) Performance on the LISP tutor seemed to improve when we introduced a facility to bring up the problem statement at any point in time, and when there is room on the screen, the problem statement is now automatically displayed. Performance in the geometry tutor seemed to improve when we introduced a facility for bringing up statements of geometry postulates at will.

(7) One of the major disadvantages of all of our tutors compared to human tutors is that, at least so far, they use only the visual medium. This means that students must move their eyes from the problem to process the textual instruction. In contrast, with a human tutor, the student can listen to the tutor while continuing to look at the problem and even have parts of the problem emphasized through the tutor's pointing.

These observations illustrate two general points about interface design for tutors:

(a) It is important to have a system that makes it clear to a student where he or she is in the problem solution and where their errors are (observations (1)–(3)).

(b) It is important to minimize working memory and processing load involved in the problem solving (observations (4)–(7)).

While one wants an interface with these properties, it is important that the interface itself be easy to learn and use. One does not want the task of dealing with the interface to come to dominate learning the subject material. An easy interface is one that minimizes the number of things to be learned and minimizes the number of actions (e.g., keystrokes, mouseclicks) that the student has to perform to communicate to the tutor. Its learnability is enhanced if it is as congruent with past experience as possible. It should also have a structure that is as congruent as possible with the problem structure. Finally, the actions should be as internally consistent as possible.

So there are clearly an important set of criteria that our tutoring efforts place on interface design. The problem is that criteria like "minimize working-memory load" or "make learning the interface easy" are not generative. To date we have dealt with interface design on an intuitive basis and on a trial and error basis. We are always left to wonder whether there is some new insight about interface design that would dramatically enhance the achievement gains displayed by a particular tutor.

4. Conclusions

What we have described is a theoretical framework for our tutoring work and some experiences based on that framework. Both the tutors and the theory are evolving objects and so it is not the case that the current embodiments of our tutors reflect all of the current insights of our theory. Still there is an approximation here and it is worthwhile to ask to what degree our tutoring experience confirmed the theory.

The first observation is that students do seem to learn from the tutors. We think this is quite a remarkable fact and not something that we had really believed would work so well when we set out to build these tutors. We have taken cognitive models of the information processing, embedded them in instructional systems, and nothing has fallen apart. They can embody substantial amounts of material, can be developed in feasible time, run within acceptable bounds of efficiency, and are robust in their behavior. The evaluations of the tutor clearly indicate that they are better than standard classroom instruction. This feasibility demonstration gives some credence to the general theoretical framework in which the tutors were built.

It is worth noting here that conventional computer-based instruction usually produces less than half of a standard deviation of improvement [15, 28]. Such instruction involves handcrafted interactions with the student in contrast to our tutors in which the interactions are generated from general principles.

It is a separate question of whether the students behave and learn with the tutors as the theory would predict. This is a difficult question to assess because the theory is probabilistic and does not specify in advance values such as the probability of encoding a production; rather these probabilities must be estimated from the data. It is also difficult because the theory only makes predictions given students' encodings of the instruction and of the problem, and students clearly vary in how they encode this information. Nonetheless, what analyses we have done do seem to confirm the theory. Figure 16 presents an analysis of some data from the LISP tutor that monitors time to type in units of code that correspond to the firing of individual productions. So for instance typing "(cons" corresponds to the firing of a production that recognizes the applicability of the CONS function. We have plotted average times associated with the firing of productions learned in lessons 2, 3, and 5 as a function of the number of times students used the production in the lesson. What these times correspond to psychologically is somewhat complex because they include a lot of low-level interactions with the tutor. However, they should reflect the

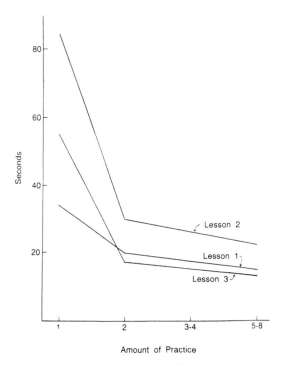

Fig. 16. Plot of learning data from the LISP tutor. Time to code the LISP symbols that are introduced in the first three lessons is plotted as a function of practice. The coding of one of these symbols corresponds to the firing of a production in the student model.

learning of the production or productions associated with the execution of the code. These learning curves have just the shape we would predict. There is a big drop in coding time from first application of a production to second as the knowledge is compiled into production form and a gradual speedup after that as the production rules become strengthened.

Another observation is that the knowledge acquired does seem to have the expected range of application. For instance, in the geometry tutor students are able to apply new combinations of the inference rules that they have learned to solve a new problem as long as the contextual heuristics that recommend the application of these rules are ones they have already encountered. On the other hand if they are presented with a problem that can be solved by the knowledge which they have been taught, but which requires applying a new contextual heuristic to see the applicability of that rule, students experience great difficulty.

Appendix A

Define the function fact. It takes a number argument, n and computes the factorial of n, which is the result of multiplying $n \times n - 1 \times n - 2 \times \cdots \times 1$. For instance, $(\text{fact } 3) = 3 \times 2 \times 1 = 6$. By definition, the factorial of 0 is 1.

(1) **(defun fact (n)**
    (cond ((equal) $\langle ACTION \rangle$**)**
       $\langle RECURSIVE\text{-}CASE \rangle$**))**

I assume that you are trying to test if the number argument is equal to the number zero. There is a special function for testing equivalence to zero. Try to use that function instead of EQUAL.

What code can you write to test if the condition for terminating case is true? Try writing a predicate.

(2) *(defun fact (n)*
    *(cond ((***zero** $\langle ACTION \rangle$*)*
       $\langle RECURSIVE\text{-}CASE \rangle$*))*

Did you mean zerop (y or n)? **y**

(3) *(defun fact (n)*
    *(cond ((***zerop n) 1**)*
       $\langle RECURSIVE\text{-}CASE \rangle$*))*

Is the value of fact in the recursive cases calculated by:

PRESS:	IF YOU WANT TO:
1	calling fact recursively with n
2	multiplying n by fact of n minus 1

    3   getting 1 2 . . . n and then multiply the results
    4   have the tutor choose

Menu choice: **3**

That is a reasonable way to think of doing factorials but it is not a plan for
a recursive function. Since you seem to be having trouble with the
recursive cases let us work through some examples and figure out the
conditions and actions for each of these cases.

  The recursive relationship is the relationship between fact called with n
and fact called with:

    PRESS: IF YOU WANT TO:
    1   n minus 1
    2   n equal to 0
    3   n plus 1
    4   have the tutor choose

Menu choice: **1**

We will consider some concrete examples. We will characterize the recursive relationship between fact called with 1 and fact called with 0.

  What is the value of (fact 1)?
  Answer: **1**

  What is the value of (fact 0)?
  Answer: **1**

    EXAMPLES
        fact (n)   fact (n − 1)
    A. (fact 1) = 1   (fact 0) = 1

We will consider some more concrete examples. We will characterize the
recursive relationship between fact called with 3 and fact called with 2.

  What is the value of (fact 3)?
  Answer: **6**

  What is the value of (fact 2)?
  Answer: **2**

    EXAMPLES
        fact (n)   fact (n − 1)
    A. (fact 1) = 1   (fact 0) = 1
    B. (fact 3) = 6   (fact 2) = 2

Since there is only one recursive case characterized by the examples you
have just worked out, the condition in this case can be just coded as T. We
will just focus on characterizing the action in this case.

In examples A and B what do you have to do to get the result of fact called with n?

PRESS: IF YOU WANT TO:
1   multiply n by one less than n
2   multiply n by fact of one less than n
3   add n to the result of fact called with one less than n
4   have the tutor choose

Menu choice: **2**

We have now worked through a series of examples that illustrate the recursive relation.
We will now return to the goal of trying to produce LISP code that specifies the recursive relation.

(4) *(defun fact (n)*
       (cond ((zerop n) 1)
              (t (fact))))

You will have to use fact at some point but right now you want to multiply.

(5) *(defun fact (n)*
       (cond ((zerop n) 1)
              (t **(times n (fact n)))))**

You cannot just code n at this point. What you want to do is subtract one from n.

(6) *(defun fact (n)*
       (cond ((zerop n) 1)
              (t (times n (fact **(difference))))))**

Difference would work in this case but it is more appropriate to use the function sub1 when you are subtracting 1 from a number.

(7) *(defun fact (n)*
       (cond ((zerop n) 1)
              (t (times n (fact **(sub1 n))))))**

— YOU ARE DONE. TYPE NEXT TO GO ON AFTER —
— TESTING THE FUNCTIONS YOU HAVE DEFINED —

THE LISP WINDOW

$\Rightarrow$ *(trace fact)*
(fact)
$\Rightarrow$ *(fact 3)*
1 ⟨Enter⟩ fact (3)

```
2 ⟨Enter⟩ fact (2)
  3 ⟨Enter⟩ fact (1)
  4 ⟨Enter⟩ fact (0)
  4 ⟨EXIT⟩ fact 1
  3 ⟨EXIT⟩ fact 1
2 ⟨EXIT⟩ fact 2
1 ⟨EXIT⟩ fact 6
6
```

REFERENCES

1. Anderson, J.R., Tuning of search of the problem space for geometry proofs, in: *Proceedings IJCAI-81*, Vancouver, BC (1981).
2. Anderson, J.R., Acquisition of cognitive skill, *Psychol. Rev.* **89** (1982) 369–406.
3. Anderson, J.R., Acquisition of proof skills in geometry, in: J.G. Carbonell, R. Michalski and T. Mitchell (Eds.), *Machine Learning: An Artificial Intelligence Approach* (Tioga, Palo Alto, CA, 1983).
4. Anderson, J.R., *The Architecture of Cognition* (Harvard University Press, Cambridge, MA, 1983).
5. Anderson, J.R., Production systems, learning, and tutoring, in: D. Klahr, P. Langley and R. Neches (Eds.), *Production System Models of Learning and Development* (MIT Press, Cambridge, MA, 1987) 437–458.
6. Anderson, J.R., Analysis of student performance with the LISP tutor, in: N. Fredericksen, R. Glaser, A. Lesgold and M. Shafto (Eds.), *Diagnostic Monitoring of Skill and Knowledge Acquisition* (Erlbaum, Hillsdale, NJ, 1989).
7. Anderson, J.R., Boyle, C.F., Farrell, R. and Reiser, B.J., Cognitive principles in the design of computer tutors, in: P. Morris (Ed.), *Modelling Cognition* (Wiley, New York, 1989).
8. Anderson, J.R., Boyle, C.F. and Yost, G., The geometry tutor, in: *Proceedings IJCAI-85*, Los Angeles, CA (1985) 1–7.
9. Anderson, J.R., Corbett, A.T. and Reiser, B.J., *Essential LISP* (Addison-Wesley, Reading, MA, 1987).
10. Anderson, J.R., Farrell, R. and Sauers, R., Learning to program in LISP, *Cognitive Sci.* **8** (1984) 87–129.
11. Anderson, J.R. and Jeffries, R., Novice LISP errors: Undetected losses of information from working memory, *Human-Computer Interaction* **22** (1985) 403–423.
12. Anderson, J.R. and Skwarecki, E., The automated tutoring of introductory computer programming, *Commun. ACM* **29** (1986) 842–849.
13. Anderson, J.R. and Thompson, R., Use of analogy in a production system architecture, in: A. Ortony et al. (Eds.), *Similarity and Analogy* (to appear).
14. Anderson, R.C., Kulhavy, R.W. and Andre, T., Conditions under which feedback facilitates learning from programmed lessons, *J. Educ. Psychol.* **63** (1972) 186–188.
15. Bangert-Drowns, R.L., Kulik, J.A. and Kulik, C.C., Effectiveness of computer-based education in secondary schools, *J. Comput.-Based Educ.* **12** (1985) 59–68.
16. Bloom, B.S., The 2 sigma problem: The search for methods of group instruction as effective as one-to-one tutoring, *Educ. Researcher* **13** (1984) 3–16.
17. Brown, J.S. and Burton, R.R., Diagnostic models for procedural bugs in basic mathematical skills, *Cognitive Sci.* **2** (1978) 155–192.
18. Brown, J.S., Burton, R.R. and de Kleer, J., Pedagogical, natural language and knowledge engineering techniques in SOPHIE I, II and III, in: D. Sleeman and J.S. Brown (Eds.), *Intelligent Tutoring Systems* (Academic Press, New York, 1982) 227–282.
19. Brown, J.S. and VanLehn, K., Repair theory: A generative theory of bugs in procedural skills, *Cognitive Sci.* **4** (1980) 379–426.

20. Carroll, J., Designing minimalist training materials, Research Rept. 46643, IBM Watson Research Center, Yorktown Heights, NY (1985).
21. Clancey, W.J., Tutoring rules for guiding a case method dialogue, in: D. Sleeman and J.S. Brown (Eds.), *Intelligent Tutoring Systems* (Academic Press, New York, 1982) 201–225.
22. Collins, A.M., Warnock, E.H. and Passafiume, J.J., Analysis and synthesis of tutorial dialogues, in: G.H. Bowen (Ed.), *Advances in Learning Motivation* (Academic Press, New York, 1975).
23. Corbett, A.T. and Anderson, J.R., Problem compilation and tutoring flexibility in the LISP Tutor, International Conference on Intelligent tutoring Systems (submitted).
24. Dulany, D.E., Carlson, R.A. and Dewey, G.I., A case of syntactical learning and judgment: How conscious and how abstract? *J. Experimental Psychol. General* **113** (1984) 541–555.
25. Ericsson, K.A. and Simon, H.A., *Protocol Analysis: Verbal Reports as Data* (MIT Press, Cambridge, MA, 1984).
26. Forgy, C.L., Rete: A fast algorithm for the many pattern/many object pattern match problem, *Artificial Intelligence* **19** (1982) 17–37.
27. Johnson, L. and Soloway, E., Intention-based diagnosis of programming errors, in: *Proceedings AAAI-84*, Austin, TX (1984).
28. Kulik, C.C., Kulik, J.A. and Shwalb, B.J., The effectiveness of computer-based adult education: A meta-analysis, *J. Educ. Comput. Res.* **2** (1986) 235–252.
29. Lewis, M.W. and Anderson, J.R., Discrimination of operator schemata in problem solving: Learning from examples, *Cognitive Psychol.* **17** (1985) 26–65.
30. Lewis, M.W., Milson, R. and Anderson, J.R., Designing an intelligent authoring system for high school mathematics ICAI: The TEACHERS APPRENTICE Project, in: G. Kearsley (Ed.), *Artificial Intelligence and Instruction: Applications and Methods* (Addison-Wesley, Reading, MA, 1990).
31. Matz, M., Towards a process model for high school algebra, in: D. Sleeman and J.S. Brown (Eds.), *Intelligent Tutoring Systems* (Academic Press, New York, 1982).
32. Norman, D.A., Categorization of action slips, *Psychol. Rev.* **88** (1981) 1–15.
33. Pirolli, P.L. and Anderson, J.R., The role of learning from examples in the acquisition of recursive programming skill, *Can. J. Psychol.* **39** (1985) 240–272.
34. Reder, L.M., Charney, D.H. and Morgan, K.I., The role of elaborations in learning a skill from an instructional text, *Memory and Cognition* **14** (1986) 64–78.
35. Reiser, B.J., Anderson, J.R. and Farrell, R.G., Dynamic student modelling in an intelligent tutor for LISP programming, in: *Proceedings IJCAI-85*, Los Angeles, CA (1985) 8–14.
36. Sleeman, D., Assessing aspects of competence in basic algebra, in: D. Sleeman and J.S. Brown (Eds.), *Intelligent Tutoring Systems* (Academic Press, New York, 1982) 185–199.
37. Sleeman, D. and Brown, J.S. (Eds.), *Intelligent Tutoring Systems* (Academic Press, New York, 1982).
38. Winograd, T., Frame representation and the declarative procedural controversy, in: D. Bobrow and A. Collins (Eds.), *Representation and Understanding* (Academic Press, New York, 1975).
39. Winston, P.H. and Horn, B.K.P., *LISP* (Addison-Wesley, Reading, MA, 3rd ed., 1984).

Understanding and Debugging Novice Programs

W. Lewis Johnson

USC/Information Sciences Institute, 4676 Admiralty Way,
Marina del Rey, CA 90292, USA

ABSTRACT

Accurate identification and explication of program bugs requires an understanding of the pro-
grammer's intentions. This paper describes a system called PROUST which performs intention-based
diagnosis of errors in novice PASCAL programs. The technique used involves generating possible
goal decompositions for the program, matching them against the program, and then proposing bugs
and misconceptions to explain the mismatches. Empirical studies of PROUST's performance show
that it achieves high performance in finding bugs in nontrivial student programs.

1. Introduction

Learning to program is a time-consuming and frustrating process for most
novice programmers. One reason for this is that they have to expend so much
effort in debugging their programs. Program bugs hinder the learning process
in two ways. First, the students are distracted from the curriculum material that
they are trying to understand when the programs that they write have bugs
unrelated to the concepts being learned. Second, novices frequently have
misconceptions about programming language syntax and semantics, which lead
to confusions when their programs behave differently from what they expect. It
is extremely difficult for novices to discover on their own the misconceptions
which account for the unexpected behavior.

Bugs need not be a hindrance to novice programmers, however. If a tutor
were to supervise the students' work and provide assistance when the students
make mistakes, then errors might even enhance the learning process. Performance errors provide a unique opportunity for the teacher to understand the
students' confusions and misconceptions [4]. Given such an understanding, the
teacher can then focus on remedying the student's problems, clearing the way
for further progress through the curriculum.

Unfortunately, it is rarely possible to provide each student in a programming
course with an individual tutor. What is needed instead is a computer program

Artificial Intelligence **42** (1990) 51–97

which can serve in the tutor's role. Such a program would analyze the students' programs, looking for bugs and bad programming style. It would then help the students overcome the misconceptions that were responsible for the incorrect code.

The process of analyzing programs for syntactic errors is well understood at this point; techniques exist which do a fairly good job of identifying syntactic errors [2, 13] and of correcting them [6, 15]. Semantic and logic errors, on the other hand, are not so easily diagnosed. Most semantic and logical error detectors focus on narrow ranges of bugs, such as uninitialized variables [10] or spelling errors [32]. These errors all share the property that one can detect them regardless of what the intended functionality of the program is. However, many logical errors result in programs which function, but which fail to compute the desired results.

This paper will argue that in order to reliably diagnose as near to the complete range of semantic and logical errors as possible, a debugging system must understand the programmer's intentions. A program is a designed artifact; as such, its design must be taken into account when analyzing it for bugs. The program has an intended function, and has been constructed in order to achieve this function. Debugging should focus on whether the intended function and design of the program are correct, and whether these intentions have been properly executed. Such an approach makes it possible to detect more bugs, and to explain better how to correct them. By relating bugs to the student's intended design, it may be possible to help students learn to design their programs better.

This paper will show that intention-based analysis can be an effective method for diagnosing bugs in programs. It requires knowledge of how to write programs, what errors novice programmers are likely to make, and some general understanding of what a given program is supposed to do. Given such knowledge, one can identify the intended function of each statement in a program, what bugs are present, and where they are manifested. A system called PROUST will be described which determines the intentions underlying novice programs and uses this understanding of intentions to perform accurate analyses of nonsyntactic bugs. The results of empirical evaluations of PROUST on student programs will be presented; these results will demonstrate the effectiveness of the approach.

1.1. Intention-based analysis of an example buggy program

To see why understanding programmers' intentions is important in diagnosing bugs, let us examine the bugs in an example novice PASCAL program. The program to be considered here is a solution to the Rainfall Problem that was assigned in an introductory PASCAL course.

Rainfall Problem. Noah needs to keep track of rainfall in the New Haven area in order to determine when to launch his ark. Write a PASCAL program that will help him do this. The program should prompt the user to input numbers from the terminal; each input stands for the amount of rainfall in New Haven for a day. Note: since rainfall cannot be negative, the program should reject negative input. Your program should compute the following statistics from this data:

(1) the average rainfall per day;
(2) the number of rainy days;
(3) the number of valid inputs (excluding any invalid data that might have been read in);
(4) the maximum amount of rain that fell on any one day.

The program should read data until the user types 99999; this is a sentinel value signaling the end of input. Do not include the 99999 in the calculations. Assume that if the input value is nonnegative, and not equal to 99999, then it is valid input data.

This problem requires that the students write a program which reads in a series of numbers, each of which represents the amount of rainfall on a particular day. Input termination is signaled when the user types the value 99999. The program is supposed to check the input for validity, compute the average and the maximum of the input, and count the total number of valid inputs and the number of positive inputs. The program must prevent the final 99999 from being included in the computations. This problem thus tests the students' ability to combine a variety of computations into a single working program.

Figure 1 shows a solution to the Rainfall Problem written by a novice programmer. We will refer to this example repeatedly throughout this paper when discussing PROUST. This program has a number of different bugs; however, there is one set of bugs that is of particular interest. Instead of there being a single loop which reads the data, processes it, and checks for 99999, there are two. One is a repeat loop, starting at line 8 and ending at line 28. The other is a while loop contained within the repeat loop. The inner while loop is an infinite loop; it tests the variable RAIN against 99999, but never modifies RAIN.

Well-known analysis techniques such as data flow analysis [10] are capable of detecting the infinite loop in the program in Fig. 1. However, if an infinite loop is a manifestation of a more significant programming error, then simply pointing out the infinite loop may distract the student away from correcting the true error. In particular, if a loop does not belong in the program at all, then the question of whether or not the loop is infinite is moot. Our empirical studies of how students debug programs indicate that novice programmers tend to correct the surface manifestations of bugs rather than the bugs themselves; thus proper descriptions of bugs are crucial.

We believe that the proper analysis of the bug in this program is as follows. The student probably did not intend the while statement at line 19 to loop at

```
1 program Rainfall (input, output);
2
3 var
4    Rain, Days, Totalrain, Raindays, Highrain, Averain: real;
5
6 begin
7    Rain := 0;
8    repeat
9       writeln ('Enter rainfall');
10      readln;
11      read (Rain);
12      while Rain < 0 do
13        begin
14           writeln (Rain:0:2, 'is not possible, try again');
15           readln;
16           read (Rain)
17        end;
18
19      while Rain <> 99999 do
20        begin
21           Days := Days + 1;
22           Totalrain := Totalrain + Rain;
23           if Rain > 0 then
24              Raindays := Raindays + 1;
25           if Highrain < Rain then
26              Highrain := Rain
27        end;
28    until Rain = 99999;
29
30    Averain := Totalrain / Days;
31
32    writeln (Days:0:0, 'valid rainfalls were entered');
33    writeln ('The average rainfall was', Averain:0:2, 'inches');
34    writeln ('The highest rainfall was', Highrain:0:2);
35    writeln ('There were', Raindays:0:0, 'in this period');
36 end.
```

Fig. 1. A buggy solution to the Rainfall Problem.

all. Instead, the effect of an if statement was intended. Since the input statements are at the top of the repeat loop, and the loop exit test is at the bottom of the repeat loop, there has to be a way for control to skip from the input statements to the end of the loop when 99999 is read. Otherwise the 99999 would be processed as if it were a rainfall amount. An if statement would serve this purpose, but the student has written a while statement instead. Empirical analyses of novice programming errors [19] have shown that novice programmers commonly confuse the meanings of if and while, particularly when they are embedded within other loops. If this bug were to be described to the novice programmer, the description should focus on the probable misconception about the meanings of if and while, rather than just on the fact that the while statement is an infinite loop.

The key difference between the above analysis and the analysis that a data flow analyzer would produce is the following. A data flow analyzer analyzes the behavior of the program itself, independent of the intentions underlying it. In the above analysis, the focus was on understanding the intentions underlying the program, and then on referring to those intentions in diagnosing bugs. Thus the bug analysis presented above is an *intention-based* analysis; a data flow analyzer, in contrast, performs non-intention-based analysis.

Figure 2 shows PROUST's output when analyzing the program in Fig. 1. The output demonstrates PROUST's ability to understand the intentions underlying the program. PROUST finds all of the bugs in the program, including the while-for-if bug. Although PROUST's output indicates the possibility that the

NOW BEGINNING BUG REPORT:

>> Now Reporting CRITICAL Bugs in the SETUP part of your program:

You left out the initializations for the variables HIGHRAIN, DRYDAYS, RAINDAYS, and TOTALRAIN. Programs should not fetch values from uninitialized variables! If you don't initialize these variables to the values that you want, you will have no way of knowing what values they will be initialized to.

(TO CONTINUE, PLEASE PRESS CARRIAGE RETURN)

>> Now Reporting MINOR Bugs in the SETUP part of your program:

The initialization at line 7 appears to be unnecessary.
The statement in question is:
    RAIN := 0

(TO CONTINUE, PLEASE PRESS CARRIAGE RETURN)

>> Now Reporting CRITICAL Bugs in the CONTROL part of your program:

You used a WHILE statement at line 19 where you should have used an IF. WHILE and IF are NOT equivalent in this context; using WHILE in place of IF can result in infinite loops.
The statement in question is:
    WHILE RAIN <> 99999 DO . . .

(TO CONTINUE, PLEASE PRESS CARIAGE RETURN)

>> Now Reporting CRITICAL Bugs in the OUTPUT part of your program:

The maximum and the average are undefined if there is no valid input. But lines 34 and 33 output them anyway. You should always check whether your code will work when there is no input! This is a common cause of bugs.

You need a test to check that at least one valid data point has been input before line 30 is executed. The average will bomb when there is no input.

BUG REPORT NOW COMPLETE.

Fig. 2. PROUST's output for the program in Fig. 1.

program will enter an infinite loop, it does not analyze the program by looking for infinite loops. Rather, it tries to understand the intended role of each component of the program, and in the process discovers a while statement that appears to have the intended function of an if statement. Once the bug is found, PROUST can then proceed to explain how the bug will be manifested in incorrect program behavior.

1.2. The principal components of intention-based diagnosis

We will now look at what a system needs in order to be able to perform an intention-based analysis such as the one that we have just seen. The particular mechanisms which PROUST uses to perform the analysis will be introduced. Further discussion of these mechanisms will appear later in the paper.

1.2.1. *Problem descriptions*

One of the things which an intention-based analysis system must do, as indicated above, is to determine what the intended function of the program is. It is difficult to infer the intended function of a program just by inspecting the program; there is no way of knowing whether the program's behavior is really what the programmer had in mind. One needs some way of forming expectations about what the program functionality ought to be. In PROUST the expectations are provided in the form of a description of the problem that was assigned to the students. It is assumed that the students' intended functionality will be reasonably close to what was stated in the problem.

Problem descriptions, for PROUST, are sets of goals to be satisfied, and sets of descriptions of the data objects that test goals apply to. Figure 3 shows one of the problem descriptions that PROUST uses, the description of the Rainfall Problem.[1] These problem descriptions define data objects which the program will manipulate, and some goals to be achieved on those objects. For example, *Output*(*Average*(?DailyRain)) specifies that the average of the rainfall inputs should be computed and output, where the rainfall input is referred to as the

?DailyRain isa Scalar Measurement.

Achieve the following goals:
    Sentinel-Controlled Input Sequence(?DailyRain, 99999);
    Input Validation(?DailyRain, ?DailyRain < 0);
    Output(*Average*(?DailyRain));
    Output(*Count*(?DailyRain));
    Output(*Guarded Count*(?DailyRain, ?DailyRain > 0));
    Output(*Maximum*(?DailyRain));

Fig. 3. The Rainfall Problem in PROUST's problem description notation.

[1] The syntax of the description has been altered to make it more readable.

object ?DailyRain. Note that goals implied by the listed goals, such as checking for division by zero when the average is computed, are omitted. Explicitly mentioned goals are more likely to match the students' intentions than implied goals, which the students often overlook or get wrong.

1.2.2. *Hypothesizing goal decompositions*

Given a problem description, the task of identifying the intentions underlying a program amounts to answering the following questions:

- How do the goals in the problem description relate to the goals that are actually implemented in the program?
- How did the programmer intend to implement these goals?

That is, general expectations about the intended function of a program must be refined into a specific account of the functionality and design of the program.

Although the problem description helps determine what the intended function of the program is, it says nothing about how that function is to be implemented. In fact there is nothing it could say, because each student is likely to implement the problem goals in a different way. In small programs it may be possible to enumerate the different ways of solving the problem, but in more complex problems such as the Rainfall Problem the number of possible solutions is too great. When an intention-based diagnosis system works in a complex domain such as PROUST's, it cannot rely solely on a canned description of possible solutions. Instead, it must be able to construct a description of the intentions underlying each individual student solution.

In order to construct descriptions of novice intentions, PROUST relies upon a knowledge base of programming plans. Programming plans, as defined by Soloway, are stereotypic methods for satisfying programming goals [29]. Rich's programming cliches serve a similar function [22]. PROUST's plan knowledge base was constructed as a result of studying commonly occurring patterns of code in PASCAL programs, and from examples culled from programming textbooks. PROUST combines these plans into possible implementations for each goal, and then matches the plans against the program. If the student's code matches one of the predicted plans, then PROUST concludes that the student's intended implementation matches fairly closely to the plan that matched.

When PROUST combines plans into predictions of how the student implemented the problem goals, it is said to be generating possible *goal decompositions* for the problem. A goal decomposition relates the goals that a program is supposed to achieve to the plans that achieve it. In the process of going from goals to plans, it may be necessary to break goals into sets of subgoals, combine related goals into a larger goal, and add goals that are not explicitly stated in the problem. For nontrivial problems, there is often a large number of possible goal decompositions.

```
write('Enter rainfall value:');
read(Rain);
while Rain <> 99999 do
   begin
      if Rain < 0 then
         writeln('Invalid input, try again');
      if Rain > 0 then
         Raindays := Raindays + 1;
      if Highrain < Rain then
         Highrain := Rain;
      if Rain >= 0 then
         begin
            Totalrain := Totalrain + Rain;
            Days := Days + 1;
         end;
      write('Enter rainfall value:');
      read(Rain);
   end
```

Fig. 4. An alternative way of combining input and input validation.

An example of where goals can be combined in different ways in the Rainfall Problem is in deciding whether the goal of inputting the rainfall data and the goal of checking it for validity should be combined. If the two goals are combined into a single plan, then a program such as the one in Fig. 1 results. There the contiguous block of code from line 10 to line 17 reads, tests, and then re-reads the data. If the *Input* goals and the *Input Validation* goal are not combined, then they may wind up in separate parts of the program, as in the example in Fig. 4.

It should be emphasized that the goal decomposition that PROUST hypothesizes for a program need not *correctly* implement the goals in the problem description. The student may have decomposed goals improperly, or have used an inappropriate plan. In such cases PROUST's goal decomposition should still reflect what the student did. PROUST's programming knowledge base is therefore extended so that it can generate incorrect goal decompositions. PROUST is thus able to predict some kinds of bugs as it constructs goal decompositions. Not all bugs are recognized in this fashion, but a significant number are.

1.2.3. *When predicted intentions fail to match*

Even though PROUST generates a number of goal decompositions for each goal, there is no guarantee that any of them will match the student's program exactly. In fact, mismatches are what most often provide clues that there are bugs in the program. If we have chosen the right goal decomposition, and it fails to match the program, then the mismatches can be explained as failed attempts on the part of the programmer to implement the goal decomposition in the code.

SENTINEL READ-PROCESS REPEAT PLAN

Constants: ?Stop
Variables: ?New
Template:
   repeat
      subgoal Input(?New)
      subgoal Sentinel Guard(?New, ?Stop, ?∗)
   until ?New = ?Stop

Fig. 5. A plan for implementing *Sentinel-Controlled Input Sequence*.

PROUST detects the possibility of a while-for-if bug in the example program by matching different goal decompositions against the program. The goal that PROUST tries to decompose is the *Sentinel-Controlled Input Sequence* goal, the goal of reading in a sequence of numbers until some designated sentinel value is reached. It constructs several goal decompositions for this goal, some using while loops, some using repeat loops; it also tries different ways of structuring the loop. The closest decomposition that it finds uses the SENTINEL READ-PROCESS REPEAT PLAN, shown in Fig. 5. PROUST first matches the repeat statement pattern in the plan against repeat statement at line 8 in the program. It then selects plans to implement the subgoals in the plan, *Input* and *Sentinel Guard*. No plan for implementing the *Sentinel Guard* subgoal matches the program. All of PROUST's plans for implementing *Sentinel Guard* require that there be an if statement to test for the sentinel value; no such if statement appears in the program.

Now, in order to make sure that the student's program is properly understood, some knowledge of common student errors is needed. We need to be able to recognize that the while loop in program could be a buggy implementation of the expected subgoal. In PROUST this knowledge is represented as a knowledge base of production rules, called *plan-difference rules*. These plan-difference rules are responsible for suggesting bugs and misconceptions which account for the mismatches. One such rule, a rule for recognizing when while statements were used in place of if statements, is paraphrased in Fig. 6. Plan-difference rules either account for the differences between the plan and the code by means of bugs and misconceptions, or suggest a way to transform the plan to make it fit the programmer's apparent intentions better.

IF a while statement is found in place of an if statement,
AND the while statement appears inside of another loop,
THEN the bug is a while-for-if bug, probably caused by
    a confusion about the control flow of embedded loops.

Fig. 6. Paraphrase of a plan-difference rule for explaining while-for-if bugs.

1.3. Summary of PROUST's approach

To summarize, intention-based errors diagnosis, as it is realized in PROUST, involves performing the following steps:

- generating hypotheses about the intentions underlying the program,
- matching these hypothesis against the code,
- explaining the mismatches.

PROUST is unique in that it can generate a range of hypotheses to test against each program, and because it uses knowledge of common bugs and misconceptions to explain mismatches.

Subsequent sections will explore the different stages of PROUST's analysis in further detail. Section 3 describes the process of constructing goal decompositions. Section 4 describes plan-difference analysis. Section 5 describes how PROUST chooses among alternative interpretations of the program. A more detailed description of each of these processes can be found in [16].

2. Comparing PROUST's Approach to Other Approaches

A number of systems have been built to analyze program errors. Virtually all of these systems are non-intention-based. Instead of identifying the programmer's intentions, they analyze the structure or behavior of the program, and then infer bugs directly from this analysis. In this section some of these other approaches will be compared against PROUST's. In general, other systems cannot recognize as wide a range of bugs, nor can they diagnose bugs as accurately. We will then look at the few systems which are capable of intention-based analysis in other domains, or in other contexts, in order to see how these systems compare with PROUST.

2.1. Non-intention-based approaches

The most common approach to finding nonsyntactic program bugs is to look for anomalous program behavior or structure. The focus here is on programs which can clearly be seen to have bugs, regardless of what the programmer's intentions were. Some systems look for anomalous data flow [10], computations that may not terminate [33], or compare the code against a catalog of common novice mistakes [30]. Others try to interpret runtime errors [14, 32]. Still others analyze program traces for surprising behavior [31]. These systems may be effective for finding certain classes of bugs, but they will not work when the program has no obvious anomalies. Furthermore, they are not very good at pinpointing where the error occurred and why. We saw this in the while-for-if bug in Fig. 1. Without any knowledge of the intended function of the faulty loop, there is no way of knowing whether the exit test of the loop is wrong, whether the body is wrong, or whether a loop was intended at all. Thus a system which looks for common anomalies will not be able to help a novice programmer realize his intentions in the code.

Another way to find bugs without knowledge of the programmer's intentions is to have the programmer say what is wrong with the program, and have the system try to trace the cause of the bug. The user describes the error by supplying test data which causes the program to generate incorrect output, and indicating the discrepancies between the desired output and the actual output. This approach is used in Eisenstadt's PROLOG Trace Package [8], and in troubleshooting systems such as FALOSY [25], E. Shapiro's debugger [27], and D. Shapiro's SNIFFER system [26]. These systems all assume that the programmer is competent enough to spot any and all incorrect behavior. This assumption is not valid for novice programmers; in fact part of what novice programmers must learn is how to test their programs systematically. A debugging system for novices should be smart enough to find bugs without depending upon the user for assistance.

2.2. Intention-based approaches

In comparison to the number of non-intention-based error diagnosis systems, the number of intention-based ones are few. Those that exist are relatively limited either in their ability to hypothesize intentions underlying programs, or in their ability to handle a wide range of programming errors.

A first step toward intention-based diagnosis is to analyze programs by comparing them against one or more ideal solutions supplied by the instructor. LAURA was an early example of the use of this approach [1]. It was given a single ideal solution for each problem, and compared student solutions against the ideal. Such an approach is acceptable if there is little variability in correct problem solutions, i.e., if the goal decompositions of solutions are essentially the same. In the programming problems that PROUST analyzes, there is simply too much variability for such a scheme to work.

TALUS [23] is another system that compares ideal solutions against programs; it compares each program against a suite of known correct algorithms. TALUS reports the differences between the student's program and the most closely matching correct algorithm. TALUS is similar to PROUST in that it analyzes programs by comparing them against hypothetical algorithms. It differs from PROUST in that all possible goal decompositions must be built in ahead of time, and because it has no knowledge about what bugs and misconceptions are likely to occur in novice programs. Thus TALUS is unlikely to perform as well as PROUST on problems where many variations in goal decompositions are possible, and where students are likely to make mistakes which obscure the intended function of the code. There is a number of different goal decompositions for the Rainfall Problem, resulting from decisions about how to check for boundary conditions, and how to combine the various goals stated in the problem. Misconceptions about the semantics of PASCAL keywords such as while, if, repeat, begin, and end can frequently result in programs with bizarre structure which is hard to relate to any correct program solution.

The LISP tutor [9] can perform intention-based analysis of errors in LISP programs. It has a model of what the student's current goals are, and updates this model whenever the student makes an edit to the program. If the student makes an incorrect edit to the program, the LISP tutor tries to understand why the student made that change, based upon the tutor's model of the student's intentions. It then corrects the student immediately.

The LISP tutor is successful at diagnosing errors, provided that it understands the programmer's intentions properly. Such an understanding is possible only if the tutor knows what goal the programmer is carrying out at each point in the task. In nontrivial programs, this can be difficult, and the LISP tutor therefore requires guidance from the student. For example, when a student is writing a recursive program using the LISP tutor, the tutor forces the user to select from among a predefined set of recursion plans. The tutor then supplies the student with a program template, which he or she fills in. Recursion plans which do not belong to the predefined set are disallowed.

The advantage of the LISP tutor's approach is that it provides the user with immediate feedback when errors are encountered. The disadvantage is that it restricts the freedom of the student in designing the program. Although PROUST cannot currently analyze recursive programs, it can analyze iterative ones, and it does not require guidance from the user to do so. PROUST also is designed to analyze programs which achieve multiple goals; it does not presume that these goals will be satisfied in any particular order. The LISP tutor is designed to handle programs which achieve a relatively small number of goals; it must assume a small number in order to be able to predict what the user's goal state might be at any given time.

The MACSYMA advisor [13] is similar to PROUST in that it critiques a novice's use of MACSYMA after the novice has attempted to solve the problem. The problems that it analyzes require fewer steps to solve than PROUST's, however. Furthermore, the MACSYMA advisor makes simplifying assumptions about the student's abilities: it assumes that the students' errors are caused only by factual misconceptions about MACSYMA commands. PROUST makes no similar assumption: it is designed to handle the bugs that novice programmers are actually observed to make, regardless of cause. The difference in assumptions results in differences between PROUST's and the MACSYMA advisor's representations of intentions, as we will see later on.

3. Goal Decompositions

This section describes PROUST's goal decompositions, and explains how they are constructed. These goal decompositions are central to PROUST: PROUST's ability to analyze student programs successfully depends upon its ability to construct goal decompositions which fit these programs. The goal decompositions constitute a model of the student's intentions, a model which is used when identifying and describing bugs. The discussion in this section will proceed as follows. First, the content and purpose of goal decompositions will be discussed. Then the knowledge used in creating these goal decompositions will be discussed. Then the knowledge used in creating these goal decompositions will be described, together with the process which creates them. Finally, the effectiveness of PROUST at recognizing the goal decompositions underlying programs will be assessed.

3.1. The contents of goal decompositions

A goal decomposition is an account of how the goals in the problem are realized in the program. It relates goals to the means by which the goals are implemented; i.e., it relates goals to subgoals and/or plans. The goal decomposition describes why each goal or subgoal arose as part of the solution, e.g., it was dictated by the problem statement, or it was implied by one of the goals in the problem statement. PROUST's goal decompositions thus indicate, for every statement in the program, what goal that statement serves to implement, and in turn how the implemented goal fits into the overall scheme for solving the problem.

In order to see what goes into PROUST's goal decompositions, let us examine the goal decomposition generated by PROUST for the example program in Fig. 1 in some detail. An analysis will be presented of the implementation of the goal *Sentinel-Controlled Input Sequence*, the goal of inputting a sequence of values until a sentinel value is read, in this program. An excerpt of the program relating to this goal appears for reference in Fig. 7.

```
 8 repeat
 9    writeln ('Enter rainfall');
10    readln;
11    read (Rain);
12    while Rain < 0 do
13      begin
14        writeln (Rain:0:2, 'is not possible, try again');
15        readln;
16        read (Rain)
17      end;
18
19    while rain <> 99999 do
20      begin
      .
      .
      .
28      end;
29 until Rain = 99999;
```

Fig. 7. An excerpt of the program in Fig. 1.

PROUST's goal decomposition for this example refers to several goals and plans, each of which will be defined below. The following goals will be referred to in PROUST's goal decomposition:

- *Sentinel-Controlled Input Sequence*: read data and process it until a sentinel value is input;
- *Input Validation*: ensure that input data is valid;
- *Input*: read a single datum;
- *Sentinel Guard*: guard against a sentinel value accidentally being processed as data.

The following plans will be used:

- SENTINEL READ-PROCESS REPEAT PLAN: a repeat loop, in which an *Input* subgoal, a *Sentinel Guard* subgoal, and a set of computations on the input are found (this plan was shown in Fig. 5);
- VALIDATED PROCESS-READ WHILE INPUT PLAN: an *Input* subgoal, followed by a while loop which tests the input for validity, and re-reads it if necessary;
- SENTINEL SKIP GUARD PLAN: an if statement test for a sentinel value.

Note that here, as in the rest of this article, names of goals appear in italics; names of plans appear in capitals.

PROUST's goal decomposition for the example program is as follows.

> The problem description includes two goals, among others: *Sentinel-Controlled Input Sequence* and *Input Validation*. The *Sentinel-Controlled Input Sequence* goal is implemented using the SENTINEL READ-PROCESS REPEAT PLAN. The *Input* subgoal of the plan is combined with the *Input Validation* goal, and the resulting goal is implemented using a VALIDATED PROCESS-READ WHILE INPUT PLAN. This plan matches lines 10 through 17 in the program. The *Sentinel Guard* subgoal of the SENTINEL READ-PROCESS REPEAT PLAN is implemented using a SENTINEL SKIP GUARD PLAN. However, there is a bug in this plan: a while statement was used instead of an if.

PROUST's account of the code in Fig. 7 maps the goals in the problem statement onto plans, and maps the plans onto the code. Each plan is a program template, often containing subgoals which have to be filled in using other plans. Some plans implement a single goal; others, such as the VALIDATED PROCESS-READ WHILE INPUT PLAN, implement more than one goal. Each plan is mapped onto particular lines in the program. The goal decomposition thus identifies the overall design of the program, and what role each statement in the program plays as part of the design. It makes no claims about how the student went about producing this design, e.g., which goals the student attempted first when solving the problem.

3.2. Knowledge used in constructing goal decompositions

In order to generate goal decompositions for novice programs, PROUST requires an extensive knowledge base describing how novices write programs.
This knowledge base contains the results of extensive empirical analyses of
programs written by novice programmers [3, 17, 19]. The knowledge base is
organized as a network of frames, one frame for each plan and goal in the
knowledge base. The knowledge base includes plans that novices frequently
use to implement programming goals, and it describes common ways in which
novice programmers reformulate goals.

3.2.1. Goal frames

Goal frames in PROUST list various properties of goals, the most important
being the possible ways of implementing the goal. When PROUST is constructing a goal decomposition incorporating a goal such as *Sentinel-Controlled Input
Sequence*, it looks up the goal frame to see what alternative implementations
are listed there. Each possible implementation is used to construct an alternative goal decomposition.

Figure 8 shows PROUST's description of the goal *Sentinel-Controlled Input
Sequence*. The possible implementations are listed in the Implementations slot of
the goal frame. Of the six implementations listed, the first four, SENTINEL
PROCESS-READ WHILE, SENTINEL READ-PROCESS WHILE, SENTINEL READ-
PROCESS REPEAT, and SENTINEL PROCESS-READ REPEAT, are all plans. One of
these, SENTINEL READ-PROCESS REPEAT, was employed in constructing the
goal decomposition in the previous section. The last two implementations are
knowledge structures called "goal reformulations," which will be described
later in this section.

The example in Fig. 8 also shows some of the other slots that goal frames
typically have. The Form and Main Variable slots define the parameters of the
goal: the Form lists all parameters that the goal can take, and the Main Variable

Sentinel-Controlled Input Sequence

Instance Of:	*Read & Process*
Form:	*Sentinel-Controlled Input Sequence*(?New, ?Stop)
Main Variable:	?New
Name Phrase:	"sentinel-controlled loop"
Outer Control Goal:	T
Implementations:	SENTINEL PROCESS-READ WHILE PLAN
	SENTINEL READ-PROCESS WHILE PLAN
	SENTINEL READ-PROCESS REPEAT PLAN
	SENTINEL PROCESS-READ REPEAT PLAN
	BOGUS YES-NO LOOP
	BOGUS COUNTER-CONTROLLED LOOP

Fig. 8. A goal.

slot indicates which parameter is the principal input or output of the goal. The Instance Of slot relates goals to more abstract goal classes that they belong to. *Sentinel-Controlled Input Sequence* belongs to the goal class *Read & Process*, which consists of those goals which perform some sort of iterative reading and processing of data. The Name Phrase slot indicates how to describe the goal to a student, in English, should there be a bug in the implementation of this goal. The Outer Control Goal slot gives an estimate of how much code is required to implement the goal; a T here indicates that the code will be one of the larger constructions in the student's program. These estimates help PROUST decide which goals to analyze first in a student's program, through a process described in detail in Section 5.

3.2.2. *Plans*

Just as there is a frame in the knowledge base for each goal, there is a frame for each plan. Currently PROUST's knowledge base comprises more than fifty plans. Each frame contains a plan template, which is a pattern of statements to match against the student's code. As we saw in the SENTINEL READ-PROCESS PLAN in Fig. 5, these templates can have subgoals embedded in them. The subgoals are added to the goal decomposition, after which PROUST generates possible goal decompositions for them in turn, which are then matched against the code. Plans thus serve a dual role in PROUST: they indicate the textual structure that the code must have, and they also indicate the supergoal-subgoal structure of the code.

Figure 9 shows the SENTINEL READ-PROCESS REPEAT PLAN, in greater detail than the version that appeared in Fig. 5. This plan frame has three slots: Constants, Variables, and Template. The Template slot contains the plan template to be matched against the program. This template consists of a repeat statement of the form repeat . . . until ?New = ?Stop. Contained within the repeat statement are two subgoals, *Input* and *Sentinel Guard*. Their position in the plan template dictates where the code implementing these goals should appear in the program. Since the *Input* subgoal is at the top of the body of the repeat loop pattern, the code that implements the subgoal should be at the top of the

SENTINEL READ-PROCESS REPEAT PLAN

Constants:	?Stop
Variables:	?New
Template:	
Mainloop:	repeat
Next:	*subgoal Input*(?New)
Internalguard:	*subgoal Sentinel Guard*(?New, ?Stop, Process: ?∗)
	until ?New = ?Stop

Fig. 9. The SENTINEL READ-PROCESS REPEAT PLAN, shown in greater detail.

student's repeat loop. The code implementing *Sentinel Guard* should immediately follow the code implementing the *Input* goal, since the *Sentinel Guard* goal immediately follows the *Input* goal in the plan.

All symbols in the plan template preceded by question marks are pattern variables. Pattern variables are bound to data in the student's program when the plan is matched. The Constants and Variables slots are used to declare pattern variables, and to indicate the kinds of data that they match. A pattern variable that is declared in the Constants slot must be bound to a fixed value; for example, the constant ?Stop is bound to 99999 in solutions to the Rainfall Problem. A pattern variable that is declared in the Variables slot must be bound to some varying quantity, e.g., a PASCAL variable. The pattern variable ?New in Fig. 9, which represents the data that the sentinel-controlled loop reads and processes, is declared variable.

As the example in Fig. 9 shows, the statement patterns in plan templates are represented in a form similar to the syntactic structure of the code. For example, the pattern for the repeat statement states specifically that a repeat statement should be matched, and not some other kind of looping statement such as a while statement. This syntactic orientation contrasts with the plan calculus of Rich [22], in which plans are represented in a programming-language-independent form. A syntax-oriented representation is used in PROUST to provide lexical cues for recognizing buggy code in which the syntactic structure is wrong. The while-for-if bug in Fig. 1 is typical here. In the course of analyzing numerous novice PASCAL programs, many programs were encountered where syntactic constructs were either used inappropriately or were misused. Here are some other examples:

- begin-end pairs are sometimes inappropriately used to indicate the boundaries of loops. They appear lexically outside of the loop, rather than inside.
- begin-end pairs are sometimes omitted entirely.
- Extra repeat statements sometimes appear at the end of a program, as if to indicate that control should branch back from that point, as in a BASIC next statement.

In order to interpret programs with bugs such as these, one needs to know exactly which syntactic keywords were used in the program, and where. Thus the relevant syntactic keywords were built into the plan templates. If a syntactic keyword is being used inappropriately, the plan will fail to match. Plan difference rules, as mentioned in Section 1.2.3, can then react to and explain the incorrect keyword usage in the context of the plan. If one were to use a more abstract plan calculus representation for plans, one would then have to maintain two different representations of the same program, one used for plan analysis and another for bug analysis.

Each significant statement or subgoal in a PROUST plan has a label attached to it. In the SENTINEL READ-PROCESS REPEAT PLAN, the repeat statement is labeled Mainloop, the *Input* subgoal is labeled Next, and the *Sentinel Guard* subgoal is labeled Internalguard. These labels are used to characterize the function of each component of the plan. There is a fixed, predefined set of plan labels which are used to annotate all plans in the knowledge base. Mainloop labels, for example, are always associated with the looping statements of plans. Plan labels differ from subgoals in that instead of characterizing the function of each plan component separately, they characterize the role that the component plays within the overall plan. For example, *Input* subgoals can be used either to initialize variables or to obtain successive values for variables. Because the *Input* subgoal in the SENTINEL READ-PROCESS REPEAT PLAN is labeled Next, rather than Init, PROUST can tell that the *Input* subgoal does not initialize ?New, but instead obtains successive values of ?New.

Not all subgoals of plans must be implemented in a specific place in the program, as the *Input* and *Sentinel Guard* subgoals of the SENTINEL READ-PROCESS REPEAT PLAN must be. Some plans leave the location of subgoal implementations unspecified. The AVERAGE PLAN, the ordinary plan for computing the average of a sequence of values, is an example of a plan which does not specify where subgoals should be found. The AVERAGE PLAN appears in Fig. 10. This plan computes the average by dividing the sum of a sequence of values by the count of the number of values in the sequence. The sequence of values is represented by the pattern variable ?New. The goal of computing the sum of a sequence of values is called *Sum*; the goal of counting the number of values is called *Count*. It does not matter where the sum and count are computed, as long as they are computed before the AVERAGE PLAN is invoked. Therefore the *Sum* and the *Count* goals are not specified as plan components; instead, they are listed as "posterior goals," i.e., goals that should be added to

AVERAGE PLAN

Variables: ?Avg, ?Sum, ?Count, ?New
Posterior Goals:
        Count(?New, ?Count)
        Sum(?New, ?Sum)
        Guard Exception(*component* Update *of goal Average*,
                      ((?Count *from goal Count*) = 0))
Exception Condition:
        (?Count *from goal Count*) = 0
Template: (*component* Mainloop *of goal Read & Process*)
        followed by:
   Update: ?Avg := ?Sum / ?Count

Fig. 10. A plan with two different kinds of subgoals.

the goal decomposition, but which are not subcomponents of the plan.[2] The third posterior goal, *Guard Exception*, requires that the average computation not be performed if the count of data items is zero. The Exception Condition slot supplies the conditions under which the results of the plan are undefined, i.e., when the count of data items is zero.

3.2.3. *Goal reformulations*

Suppose that a student fails to follow the problem requirements strictly, and writes a program which reads a fixed number of inputs, rather than reading until 99999 is typed. Such slight deviations in program goals occur with some regularity in programs written by novices. In order to understand such a program, PROUST much recognize that the student's goals deviate from the problem description. Goal reformulations are used to predict and characterize such deviations.

In general, goal reformulations substitute one set of goals for another set of goals. The new goals may or may not be equivalent to the old goals. PROUST's goal for reading and processing a fixed number of inputs is called *Counter-Controlled Input Sequence*, reflecting the fact that a counter-variable is used as the loop control variable in such cases. PROUST reformulates its *Sentinel-Controlled Input Sequence* goal into a *Counter-Controlled Input Sequence* goal in order to construct an accurate goal decomposition for the student's program. Since the student's goal is inappropriate for the problem the goal decomposition must be marked as buggy.

Goal reformulations such as the one going from *Sentinel-Controlled Input Sequence* to *Counter-Controlled Input Sequence* are stored in PROUST's knowledge base as goal reformulation frames. Two of the six implementations for *Sentinel-Controlled Input Sequence*, BOGUS YES-NO LOOP and BOGUS COUNTER-CONTROLLED LOOP, are goal reformulation frames. Figure 11 shows one of

BOGUS COUNTER-CONTROLLED LOOP

Form:
    BOGUS COUNTER-CONTROLLED LOOP(?New, ?Stop)
Component Goals:
    Counter-Controlled Input Sequence(?Cnt, ?New, ?Max)
Bugs:
    Implements Wrong Goal(⟨Lisp code for further describing bug⟩)

Fig. 11. A buggy reformulation of *Sentinel-Controlled Input Sequence*.

---

[2] The word "posterior" is used because the goals are added to the goal decomposition after the plan template has been matched. This is an efficiency consideration, to ensure that no further development of the goal decomposition is performed until PROUST has determined that the current plan template matches the code.

these, the BOGUS COUNTER-CONTROLLED LOOP reformulation. The reformulation frame contains two principal slots: a Component Goals slot, which lists the goals which will replace the old goals, and a Bugs slot, which describes the bug associated with this goal reformulation. The bug description indicates that the student is implementing the wrong goal; the details of the bug description are provided by a piece of LISP code that is not shown here. Such goal reformulation frames are examples of buggy novice "knowledge" about programming, used to characterize common flaws in novice goal decompositions.

Another example of goal reformulation appeared in the goal decomposition of the program in Fig. 1. There the goals *Input* and *Input Validation* were combined into single goal, implemented using the VALIDATED PROCESS-READ WHILE INPUT PLAN. This is done by first reformulating the two goals into a single goal, called *Validated Input*, and then looking for a plan to implement that goal. To handle cases such as this, reformulation rules are associated with goals such as *Input* and *Input Validation* in the knowledge base. Such rules fire when a goal is being decomposed while other related goals are active, suggesting ways of regrouping the goals.

3.3. Constructing and matching goal decompositions

The discussion will now turn from the knowledge used in goal decompositions to the process of constructing goal decompositions and matching them against the student's code. This process involves searching a state space called the *interpretation space*. The term "interpretation" will be used in this article to refer to the entire body of information gained when analyzing a student's program. The current discussion focuses on two parts of interpretations, goal decompositions and the mapping between goal decompositions and the students' code.

Each state in the interpretation space includes three things:

- an agenda of goals whose implementation in the program has yet to be determined,
- a partial goal decomposition,
- matches between the plans in the partial goal decomposition and the code.

In the initial state, the goal agenda is exactly those goals which are listed in the problem description, and the partial goal decomposition is empty. In the final state, the goal agenda is empty, and the goal decomposition is completely specified. As PROUST traverses the state space, it incrementally elaborates the goal decomposition and matches the plans in the goal decomposition against the program.

The following types of transitions are performed between states:

- goal selection: a goal is selected from the goal agenda;

- goal reformulation: the selected goal, possibly together with other goals, is reformulated;
- plan selection and matching: the selected goal is implemented using a plan, and the plan is matched against the program. Any subgoals in the plan are added onto the goal agenda.

PROUST goes through a cycle of these transitions, alternately selecting goals and either selecting and matching plans or reformulating goals. The set of states that PROUST passes through, together with the transitions between them, constitute a tree, called the *interpretation tree*. The interpretation tree is implemented literally in PROUST as a tree of nodes, each representing a different state in the interpretation space.

The construction of the interpretation tree for the Rainfall Problem begins as follows. PROUST starts by selecting the goal *Sentinel-Controlled Input Sequence*. Then possible goal decompositions involving *Sentinel-Controlled Input Sequence* are identified. From the goal frame for *Sentinel-Controlled Input Sequence* shown in Fig. 8, PROUST finds that there are four possible plans: SENTINEL PROCESS-READ WHILE, SENTINEL PROCESS-READ WHILE, SENTINEL READ-PROCESS REPEAT, and SENTINEL PROCESS-READ REPEAT. There are also two possible buggy goal reformulations: BOGUS YES-NO LOOP and BOGUS COUNTER-CONTROLLED LOOP. PROUST therefore constructs six new interpretation states, four for the plans and two for the reformulations, and links them to the current state. Each state includes an agenda of goals remaining to be processed. In the case of the plan selection states, the goal agenda is the original goal agenda minus *Sentinel-Controlled Input Sequence*. For the goal reformulation states, the agenda also includes the new goals added as a result of the goal reformulation. In the case of the BOGUS COUNTER-CONTROLLED LOOP state, for example, the goal agenda contains the added goal *Counter-Controlled Input Sequence*, which is supposed to be implemented in place of *Sentinel-Controlled Input Sequence*.

The interpretation tree must be expanded until PROUST has identified alternative plans to match against the program. It is through matching the plans that PROUST determines whether or not a particular interpretation fits the student's program. Therefore the goal reformulation states must be expanded, using the same procedure of goal selection, goal reformulation, and plan selection. In the case of the BOGUS COUNTER-CONTROLLED LOOP state, the new goal *Counter-Controlled Input Sequence* is selected. Plans implementing this goal are retrieved. This expansion process continues until every leaf in the interpretation tree is a plan selection state.

Once a set of alternative plans are selected, each plan is matched against the program. Information is added to each interpretation tree node indicating where the plan matched the program, and whether there were any matching errors. At most one match is recorded for each plan. This means that if a plan matches the program in two places, the node in the tree for that plan must first be copied. Each copy is then annotated to indicate what part of the program it was matched against. When matching the example in Fig. 7, SENTINEL READ-PROCESS REPEAT is one of the plans that is matchable. As was shown in Fig. 9, the matchable part of the plan is the repeat loop; it matches just one statement, the repeat statement at line 8. No node splitting is necessary. In order to complete matching the plan, however, the plan subgoals must be interpreted as well. The interpretation tree expansion therefore continues, this time for each subgoal of the plans that have matched successfully.

Once PROUST has tried each of the alternative plan matches, there will usually be a single plan that matches better than the alternatives. Deciding which match is best is an involved process, which will be described in detail in Section 5. For now let it suffice to say that the goodness of match depends upon how close the match is, whether or not the mismatches can be explained as bugs, and whether the plans' subgoals were interpreted successfully. Then the node describing the best match is selected for further expansion; a new goal is selected, and the process repeats. If PROUST is unable to choose between two alternatives, it will try to back up and select a different goal. In the example in Fig. 9, no backup is necessary; the SENTINEL READ-PROCESS REPEAT PLAN matches better than any of its alternatives. Therefore expansion continues from the point in the tree where the matching of SENTINEL READ-PROCESS REPEAT and its subgoals was completed.

3.4. Goal selection and the ambiguity problem

When PROUST constructs goal decompositions it must be sensitive to problems that the plan matcher may have in matching the plans in the goal decomposition against the code. If a plan is matched without any knowledge of where in the program it should match, there is risk of ambiguous matching. The plan may match more than one section of the program, and PROUST will have no way of knowing which match is the right one. Some simple examples are plans for inputting and outputting data. All input statements and output statements look much alike. PROUST does not attempt to parse variable names or interpret output messages in order to determine what data a given input or output statement is manipulating. Therefore PROUST avoids matching input and output plans until it knows what data the variables in the program refer to.

Match ambiguity results in excessive search of the space of interpretations; since PROUST cannot tell which is the correct match for a plan, it must explore all possibilities. PROUST's plan matcher is designed to take advantage of information gained in interpreting one part of a program when matching plans in other parts of the program. PROUST orders the selection of goals to allow the plan matcher to take maximal advantage of available information about the program, thus minimizing the problem of ambiguity.

3.4.1. *Using context to reduce ambiguity*

Contextual information is supplied to the plan matcher in two ways. First, plans can refer to labeled components of other plans. Second, parameters of goals can be used to bind pattern variables in the plans that implement the goal. The COUNTER PLAN in Fig. 12 can make use of both kinds of contextual information. This plan is the common method for implementing the goal of counting a sequence of values, called *Count*. The template in this plan refers to the component labeled Process of a *Read & Process* goal. The Process component of a *Read & Process* goal is the part of the plan where the data is processed. The COUNTER PLAN states that the counter update must lie inside the Process part of the loop, thus restricting where the plan matcher must look for matches. The COUNTER PLAN has one pattern variable ?Count; this stands for the counter variable. The goal of counting values, *Count*, has two parameters, ?New, which is the quality being counted, and ?Count, which is the resulting count. The parameter bindings in the goal are passed on to the plan. Therefore if PROUST believes that the counter variable is represented by a specific PASCAL variable, say Days, this variable is supplied as a parameter to the goal, e.g., the goal might read *Count*(Rain, Days). The binding of ?Count to days is passed on to the plan, so the statement pattern ?Count := ?Count + 1 becomes Days := Days + 1.

The degree of ambiguity in matching a plan thus depends crucially upon whether or not bindings for plan variables are known beforehand. In the COUNTER PLAN example, the scope of search through the program can be reduced if we know where the *Read & Process* goal is implemented. The counter update can be spotted if we know beforehand what the counter variable is. Otherwise the plan would match any increment statement anywhere in the program.

The ambiguous match of the COUNTER PLAN can be avoided if the plan is matched after the *Sentinel-Controlled Input Sequence* and *Average* goals are analyzed. The *Sentinel-Controlled Input Sequence* goal is a *Read & Process* plan, so once a plan implementing it is matched, the plan matcher can locate the counter update in the body of the loop. The analysis of the *Average* goal provides a binding for the pattern variable ?Count. When PROUST analyzes the average computation, say Averain := Totalrain/Days, it matches it against the

Variables:	?Count
Template:	
Init:	?Count := 0
	(*in component* Process *of goal* Read & Process)
Update:	?Count := ?Count + 1

Fig. 12. The COUNTER PLAN.

pattern ?Avg := ?Sum/?Count in the AVERAGE PLAN, shown in Fig. 10. Each of the pattern variables in this pattern is bound; in particular, ?Count is bound to Days. The plan indicates that the binding of ?Count should subsequently be used when matching the *Count* goal. Thus when the *Count* goal is analyzed later on, the possibility of ambiguous plan matching is reduced.

3.4.2. *Goal selection strategies to reduce ambiguity*

The success of PROUST in reducing match ambiguity depends upon whether or not it can select goals for analysis in an order so as to take maximal advantage of previous match bindings. It employs the following strategies:

(1) select first those goals which are implemented using large plans,
(2) try to select goals whose parameters are all bound,
(3) try to select goals which do not have potential plan-matching conflicts with other goals on the agenda.

The first of these strategies is responsible for PROUST selecting *Sentinel-Controlled Input Sequence* first for decomposition. The goal frame for *Sentinel-Controlled Input Sequence* indicates that the goal is an outer control goal, i.e., it should match a major control structure in the program, such as a loop. Such major control structures are more likely to appear uniquely in the program, so ambiguity is less of a concern with them. The second and third strategies ensure that the *Count* goal is not selected until the parameters of the goal are all bound. The problem description contains two goals, *Count* and *Guarded-Count*, which are similar to each other, in that they both update counters. Therefore there are potential plan-matching conflicts between these two goals: a plan implementing one goal might match code implementing the other goal. The *Average* goal, however, has no such potential for conflict; plans for implementing the goal are clearly distinct from plans for implementing the other goals. Therefore PROUST favors selection of the *Average* goal over selection of either the *Count* goal or the *CountPositives* goal. Once the *Average* goal has been matched, the parameters of the *Count* goal are all bound to variables in the student's program, so it is now possible to select that goal without worrying about ambiguous matches.

4. Analyzing Plan Differences

If all goes well, the goal decomposition construction process outlined above will succeed in matching a goal decomposition against the student's program. Usually, however, none of PROUST's proposed goal decompositions matches exactly. The match failure can be due to an unexpected bug, or due to an unexpected variant of a plan. The differences between an expected plan and the actual code are called *plan differences*. Most of PROUST's ability to diagnose bugs comes from knowledge of how to explain these plan differences.

In what follows, PROUST's knowledge about plan differences, in the form of plan-difference rules, will be described, together with the mechanism that PROUST uses to invoke plan-difference rules.

4.1. Why plan-difference analysis is needed

Plan differences can arise for the following reasons.

- A goal was improperly implemented, resulting in a bug.
- A goal was implemented in an unusual way, but correctly.

In PROUST, plan-difference rules are used to account for both kinds of plan differences. Some rules simply recognize common plan differences, and describe the bugs or misconceptions that would cause them. Others transform the matched plan into a form that corresponds more closely to the student's implementation, or transform the student's code to make the underlying goal decomposition clearer. PROUST applies plan-difference rules in succession until all plan differences are accounted for. The catalogue of plan-difference rules was constructed as a result of hand analysis of numerous novice PASCAL programs, as described in [19].

We have already seen an example of a plan-difference rule that applies to recognize an improper implementation: the while-for-if bug rule in Fig. 6. Figure 13 shows an example of a correct, but unusual, implementation, which results in a plan difference. In this example, the plans for computing the maximum and the sum have been combined: the sum update is embedded inside the if statement in the maximum computation. This sort of combination of plans occurs fairly frequently in novice programs. When PROUST tries to analyze this code, its plan predictions will fail. PROUST needs to recognize that its plans for computing the maximum and the sum are really applicable here, although they have been combined in an unusual way. PROUST also must recognize that the code is correct, albeit stylistically dubious.

The plan-difference rule in this case is called the Distribution Transformation Rule. It extracts the update statements out of the if statement and combines them into a single statement. The mechanism for doing this is as follows. As described in Section 3.3, PROUST constructs a tree of interpretation of the program. This tree serves as a database context mechanism. PROUST can

```
if Max > New then
    begin
      Max := New;
      Sum := Sum + New;
    end else
      Sum := Sum + New;
```

Fig. 13. A variant computation of the sum and maximum of a variable.

```
While (New < 9999) and (New <=0) do
  begin
    Count := Count + 1;
    Sum := Sum + New;
    if 0 < New then
      Rainy := Rainy + 1;
    if New > Max then
      Max := New;
    Writeln('Next value please:');
    Read(New);
  end
```

Fig. 14. Buggy code subject to various possible rule applications.

add assertions about the program to a given node in the tree; these assertions will only be retrievable from that node or one of its descendents. The structure of the program itself is represented as a collection of facts about each statement in the program, facts which can be superceded by subsequent assertions. The Distribution Transformation Rule simply asserts that the two running total statements are below the if statement. It also deletes one of the two statements from the list of statements remaining to be interpreted in the program. Then when the plan is rematched, it matches only one running total update, which now appears in the right position.

Finally, consider a more complex example, the buggy loop in Fig. 14. The while loop here has three bugs:

(1) it uses 9999 rather than 99999 as the sentinel value,
(2) it tries to validate the input and perform an exit test at the same time,
(3) its input validation test is incorrect; it throws out positive data rather than throwing out negative data.

The solution also has a legal variant on the predicted plan: it treats any value greater than or equal to 99999 as a sentinel value. In the predicted plan, 99999 must be typed exactly for the loop to terminate, but the sentinel test in this example is still considered to be satisfactory. PROUST can successfully analyze this code by applying a series of plan-difference rules, one for each observed difference between the predicted plan and the code.

4.2. Plan-difference rules

Plan-difference rules are test-action pairs. The test part matches a plan difference, as well as the context in which the plan difference occurred. The action part accounts for the difference in terms of bugs, plan variants, and misconceptions.

Figure 15 shows one of PROUST's plan-difference rules, the rule for detecting typographical errors in numbers. This rule is trivial in comparison to other

Number Spelling Error Rule

Error Patterns:	((∗Const∗ . ∗Const∗))
Test Code:	(SpellCorrectible (ErrorPattern) (ErrorMatched))
Bug:	(Typo (FoundStmt . , (Match-Node (BuggyMatch)))
	(ExpectedExpr . , (ErrorPattern))
	(FoundExpr . , (ErrorMatched))
	(InterpNode . , ∗InterpNode∗)))

Fig. 15. A rule for identifying typographical errors.

rules such as the Distribution Transformation Rule; its simplicity makes it that much easier to explain. The rule is represented in a frame-like manner, where some slots describe tests to be performed, and some slots describe actions to be performed. A variety of slots are specifiable as parts of plan-difference rules; this particular rule has only three slots. The Error Patterns slot characterizes the plan difference that the rule applies to. The plan difference is described as a dotted pair, where the car of the pair is what the plan predicted, and the cdr is what was actually found. Here the error pattern refers to a plan difference in which a constant was expected, e.g., 99999, and a different constant was found, e.g., 9999. The Test Code slot is a fragment of LISP code to further test applicability of the rule; this test code fragment checks whether the found constant is plausibly a typographical error. The Bug slot is part of the action part of the rule: it contains a pattern for the bug description to be generated to account for the plan difference. The pattern contains fragments of LISP code which are evaluated at the time when the rule fires; values that are generated become slot fillers for the new bug description.

Rules such as the one in Fig. 15 are so simple because their role is only to acknowledge that the bug is a known bug. The hard work has already been done in the goal decomposition and plan matching. The more complex rules are the ones that transform the code, such as the Distribution Transformation Rule. In these cases, however, the action part of the rule is represented procedurally; a LISP procedure modifies the plan, or makes local assertions about the structure of the program. It would be desirable to implement a more declarative formalism for describing these rule actions.

4.2.1. Test parts of plan-difference rules

The plan differences themselves are actually only a small part of what plan-difference rules test for. Altogether, the following kinds of information are used by plan-difference rules:

- plan differences,
- the plan component being matched,
- the plan and goal currently being analyzed, as well as those which have been analyzed previously,

– the structure of the code being matched, or its intended structure,
– bugs and misconceptions which have so far been identified.

Rules can examine the context of the plan in the program, and examine other bugs which have so far been found, in order to select the best interpretation of the plan difference. In general, plan-difference rules need to make use of any information which might shed light on the student's intentions and likely bugs.

The term patterns of plan-difference rules are written primarily in a declarative form. The plan difference, the plan component being matched, and the plan and goal being analyzed all go into the declarative pattern. However, since such a wide range of information must be tested in plan-difference rules, the declarative test-pattern language cannot be used to describe all tests that may be needed. Therefore LISP procedures are also required to perform some of the special-purpose tests, such as the test to see whether a plan difference is a plausible typographical error.

4.2.2. *Action parts of plan-difference rules*

The action parts of plan-difference rules do three kinds of things:

– suggest bugs and misconceptions,
– modify the current plan to make it fit the student's code better,
– indicate how the code should be rephrased to make the student's intentions clearer.

When bugs and misconceptions are suggested, they are added as assertions to PROUST's interpretation tree. PROUST can then see for each goal and plan what bugs and misconceptions arose in their implementation. When it is ready to describe the bugs to the student, PROUST traverses the interpretation tree from the leaf to the root, collecting all of the bug and misconception assertions that it finds there. It then can generate explanations for each bug and misconception to present to the student.

If a rule suggests that the student's plan is a variant on PROUST's plan, the plan-difference rule modifies PROUST's plan to fit the student's code better. For example, consider the test in the maximum computation in Fig. 13:

```
if New > Max then . . .
```

The test which appears in PROUST's MAXIMUM PLAN is slightly different:

```
if ?Max < ?New then . . .
```

The test predicate is reversed from what PROUST expected. A plan-difference rule is required to explain the difference. The rule which applies in this case is a rule to invert relational expressions, turning expressions of the form ?x < ?y into expressions of the form ?y > ?x. This rule is applied to the plan being matched, the MAXIMUM PLAN, changing the expected test in the plan. The plan is then matched a second time; the second time the plan matches.

Plan-difference rules sometimes suggest ways of rephrasing in the student's code to make the underlying intentions clearer. The while-for-if bug in Fig. 1 requires such a rephrasing. Once PROUST determines that the student intended the effect of an if statement, it must make an assertion in the interpretation tree indicating that the while statement should be interpreted as if it were an if statement. Then the analysis of the remaining code in the loop will not be thrown off by the extra while statement. The same mechanism is used by the Distribution Transformation Rule to handle the merged maximum and running total plans in Fig. 13.

4.3. Application of plan-difference rules

PROUST's plan-difference rule application mechanism must apply those rules which help explain plan differences, and avoid rules which do not contribute to an explanation. It must be able to chain rules and consider alternative rules to apply, but avoid blind application of rules. The example in Fig. 14 will be used to illustrate the kinds of rule application that must be permitted and the kinds that should be avoided. As indicated earlier, the loop exit test, (New < 9999) AND (New <=0), has multiple bugs. Several plan-difference rules must be applied together in order to account for the plan differences. Suppose that one of the while loop plans implementing *Sentinel-Controlled Input Sequence* is being matched, so that a test such as New <> 99999 is expected. First, a rule called the conjoined Loop Bug Rule applies, which suggests that the exit test of the loop is performing two tests at once, which are combined using an AND operator. The actual sentinel-control test should be one of the two clauses of the AND expression. It is not possible for the rule to tell which clause is the desired one, since there are other plan differences involved. Therefore the rule proposes two ways of rephrasing the test in the plan, ((New <> 99999) and ??) and (?? and (New <> 99999)).[3] The plan-difference rule applier then tries matching these new patterns against the code.

When each of the new plan patterns are matched, new plan differences arise. The first pattern fails to match because New < 9999 was found instead of New <> 99999. The second pattern fails to match because New <=0 was found instead of New <> 99999. The second of these matches is a dead end; there is no rule that can relate New <=0 to New <> 99999. Rules can be applied to explain the plan difference of the other pattern, however. A rule called the Sloppy Sentinel Guard Bug Rule applies which suggests that the student may be testing for any value greater than or equal to the sentinel value, rather than

---

[3] ?? in these patterns is a wild-card pattern variable, matching an arbitrary expression.

testing for the exact sentinel value. The Number Spelling Error Rule explains the difference between the expected 99999 and the actual 9999 as a typographical error. The plan differences are now all accounted for, so the bugs that were found are recorded in the interpretation tree. If any of the plan differences had been left unaccounted for, the entire plan-difference analysis would be scrapped, and PROUST would have to try matching a different plan against the program.

We see in this example that PROUST sometimes has to apply multiple plan-difference rules in succession, yet it cannot be certain that a given rule is applicable until the plan-difference analysis as a whole succeeds. When the Conjoined Loop Bug Rule applies, it can suggest that one of the conjuncts of the and clause is the sentinel test, but it cannot determine which one is the sentinel test. If too many rules suggested too many patterns to try, there would be a multitude of blind alleys in the plan-difference analysis. Such blind application of rules must be avoided if PROUST is to complete its analysis in a reasonable amount of time.

In order to restrict unnecessary rule application, PROUST's rule application mechanism implements the following policies. First, a constraint relaxation approach is used. Each rule is given a ranking. This ranking takes into account whether or not the rule identifies bugs, and the severity of the misconceptions that cause the bugs. It also takes into account whether the rule attempts to explain the plan differences in a statement which has already been matched, or whether it causes the plan matcher to search elsewhere in the program for possible matches. Those rules which do not presume bugs and which apply to existing partial matches are attempted first; then if necessary rules involving progressively more serious bugs and which involve greater amounts of search of the program are considered. Thus the constraints on rule application are progressively lifted until a suitable explanation is found. Similar constraint relaxation schemes have been employed in other debugging systems such as Davis' [7].

The other policy which PROUST's plan-difference rule application mechanism follows is to apply only those rules which appear to help explain the plan differences. PROUST counts the number of syntactic differences between the pattern and the matched statement, and applies only those rules which reduce this number. The rule may still be inappropriate, because the new plan differences are unexplainable; if so, then backtracking will be necessary. Nevertheless, most unnecessary rule applications are avoided by means of this restriction.

Constraining rule application in the manner described above has a price, in terms of missed bug diagnoses. The correct diagnosis is not always the most constrained one, and the correct rule to apply does not always produce an immediate improvement in the plan differences. PROUST may ultimately be forced to apply a wider range of rules in order to achieve greater diagnostic accuracy. The author has experimented with an alternative approach to rule application, which terminates rule application only when loops appear in the sequence of rules. This approach appears to do a significantly better job of finding valid explanations for plan differences, without substantially increasing the number of unnecessary rule applications.

4.4. Bug descriptions

When a plan-difference rule identifies a bug, it generates a *bug description* characterizing what kind of bug or misconception it is, and the context in which it occurred. These bug descriptions are subsequently used to generate diagnostic explanations for the student. A pattern for a bug description appeared in the plan-difference rule shown in Fig. 15. There are two types of representations which PROUST uses for describing bugs. Superficial representations are used when PROUST is able to locate and characterize the plan difference, but cannot identify the cause simply by looking at the code. Deeper representations are used when PROUST can describe the bug as an error in the student's goal decomposition, or as a misconception.

4.4.1. *Superficial bug descriptions*

Superficial bug descriptions in PROUST use the notations in "Bug collection I" [19] for describing bugs. In this system, the bugs are classified as being either missing plan components, spurious plan components, misplaced plan components, or malformed plan components. The plan components themselves are characterized according to the fucntion that they perform, i.e., initialization, input, output, update, guard, or nonexecutable statement. The function of the plan component comes from the label assigned to that component in the plan, as described in Section 3.2.2.

If PROUST describes a bug using this superficial categorization, it cannot give a very insightful description of the bug to the student. However, the categorization is still useful to PROUST when PROUST compares bugs. For example, when PROUST finds that an initialization is missing, it checks to see whether other initializations are missing. If all initializations are found to be missing, then PROUST can suggest a misconception to the student which explains all of the missing initializations at once. This allows PROUST to generate diagnostic text such as the following:

> You left out the initializations for the variables Highrain, Drydays, Raindays, and Totalrain. Programs should not fetch values from uninitialized variables! If you don't initialize these variables to the values that you want, you will have no way of knowing what values they will be initialized to.

4.4.2. *Deeper bug descriptions*

If a likely explanation for a bug can be found, PROUST describes the bug in terms of that explanation. The following explanatory descriptions of bugs are used:

– Implements Wrong Goal: Some goal was implemented in the program other than the one required by the problem statement. For example, if a student writes a counter-controlled loop instead of a sentinel-controlled loop, this is classified as an Implements Wrong Goal bug.

– Wrong Plan for Goal: The student's plan for implementing a goal is not a recommended one. For example, it may have an unwanted side-effect, such as clobbering a variable which is used later on in the program.

– Misconception: The student's code indicates the presence of a specific misconception. There has to be evidence of a misconception in more than one place in the program for PROUST to classify it as a misconception. This category is further subcategorized according to type of misconception involved. The misconceptions that PROUST can recognize are described in [16]. Examples of the kind of misconceptions that PROUST recognizes are misconceptions about how control flows through while loops, and misconceptions about when variables must be initialized.

– Implements Wrong Goal Argument: A goal is implemented in the student's code, but one of the parameters of the goal is incorrect. For example, an *Input Validation* goal might perform the wrong validity test on the input data.

– Improper Contingent Goal: A goal was implemented contingently, and this resulted in a bug, because one or more cases were overlooked where the goal needed to be implemented. Contingent goal realization is described in [16].

– Wrong Component for Plan: The student's plan for implementing a goal contains a component which is appropriate to a different plan. For example, the student might write a counter-update instead of a running total update.

– Mistransformed Code: The student attempted to transform a plan, e.g., merge a RUNNING-TOTAL PLAN and a MAXIMUM PLAN as in Fig. 13. If the merged code does not work correctly, it is described as mistransformed code.

– Typo: The student made a typographical error.

4.4.3. *Reporting bug descriptions*

After the analysis of a program is complete, the bug descriptions which were created during analysis are collected and reported to the student. First, the bug descriptions are sorted according to the severity of the bug, and the part of the program in which the bug occurs. Then for each bug, an English description is generated. The English is generated using an ordinary phrasal generator, which selects a phrase to generate based upon the type of the bug and the slot fillers of the bug. Blank fields in the phrase are filled in with the names of goals, the line numbers at which statements occur, the names of variables, and other information which might supply context for the bug. We are also experimenting with other, nontextual methods for describing bugs, e.g., presenting test data which will cause the bug to manifest itself as invalid input-output behavior.

4.5. Factors influencing the form of PROUST's interpretations

We have now examined each component of the interpretations that PROUST constructs for programs. These interpretations contain a variety of information; altogether, they may include the following:

- a goal decomposition,
- matches of the plans in the goal decomposition against the code,
- bugs,
- differences between the intended function of individual statements and the actual function of these statements,
- possible misconceptions.

This information fits into the following general categories:

- what the programmer did in solving the problem,
- what the programmer was trying to do,
- flaws in his/her knowledge which resulted in problem-solving errors.

These same types of information are found in the student models that many intelligent computer-aided instruction (ICAI) systems generate. All ICAI systems to varying degrees attempt to characterize the student's program-solving process, and the knowledge that underlies this process. ICAI systems tend to differ, however, in how they describe student's knowledge and problem solving. The following will point out some of the differences between PROUST's program interpretations and student models in other systems, and will show how these differences result from characteristics of PROUST's domain.

One major difference between PROUST's diagnostic task and that of other ICAI systems is that PROUST must derive its model of the student from a single program. Systems in the subtraction domain, such as DEBUGGY [5], and in the algebra domain, such as PIXIE [28], tend to work off of a series of student solutions. When multiple problems are analyzed in succession, bug hypotheses derived from one problem can be tested by assigning the student another related problem. The system can then check whether the student solves the new problem as the bug hypothesis would predict. In PROUST's domain, however, it is not practical to assign multiple problems to students and then analyze the bugs afterwards. Each programming problem requires substantial effort on the part of the programmer, and programmers want immediate feedback concerning their program before starting a new one. Thus it is incumbent upon PROUST to analyze the student's errors and give feedback as soon as possible, even if the underlying causes of the bugs are not yet clear to PROUST.

One consequence of the fact that PROUST models the intentions underlying a single program is that it often cannot distinguish what the programmer does in the specific case from what the programmer does in general. If a program has a bug, it may result from an accidental error such as a typographical error, or it may result from a deep-seated misconception. Distinguishing the two explanations requires looking for repeated occurrences of the same bug. If a bug occurs just once, it is likely to be an accidental error; if it occurs consistently, a misconception may be implicated.

PROUST does have one means for checking whether bugs occur systematically; it can check whether the same bug occurs more than once in the same program. The programming problems that we assign students tend to have multiple goals; PROUST can compare the implementation of similar goals to look for systematic errors. If, for example, all initializations are missing from a program, then there is strong evidence that the programmer has a misconception about initializing variables. In simpler domains such as subtraction or algebra there is less opportunity for the same bug to occur more than once within the same problem solution. Thus systematicity of errors within a single program can compensate in part for the lack of a suite of problems to analyze.

When ICAI systems try to model student behavior, they either trace student errors to incorrect problem-solving procedures or to factual misconceptions about the domain. Subtraction systems such as DEBUGGY are good examples of systems that identify incorrect problem-solving procedures. Genesereth's MACSYMA advisor [11] and Clancey's proposed GUIDON-2 system are examples of systems which focus on factual misconceptions. The systems that focus on factual misconceptions, unlike PROUST or DEBUGGY, make strong simplifying assumptions about the student's problem-solving ability. The MACSYMA advisor is a case in point. In the MACSYMA advisor, there is an explicit model of a student problem solver, called MUSER; this same problem solver is used both to solve problems and to model the student solving problems. The advisor assumes that if a student uses MACSYMA incorrectly, it can only be because the student's factual knowledge about how individual MACSYMA commands work is incorrect. The appropriateness of this assumption cannot be assessed without empirical analyses of how novice MACSYMA users actually behave; the advisor appears to be based upon observations of only a handful of students.

In contrast to the MACSYMA advisor and GUIDON-2, PROUST makes fewer assumptions about the student's problem-solving procedure. PROUST assumes that the student's program can be analyzed in terms of goals, but there is no requirement that the goals be decomposed as an expert would. A student might not realize that programmers have to worry about boundary conditions, for example, and still produce a program with a recognizable goal decomposition. Such a student cannot be said to have the same problem-solving procedure as expert programmers, since part of what an expert does is to check systematically for boundary conditions.

This weakening of the assumptions about the student's problem-solving behavior has serious repercussions for error diagnosis. It means that it is not always possible to trace bugs back to the student's factual knowledge. Any given bug may be caused by a factual misconception, a flaw in the student's problem-solving procedure, a failure to follow the problem requirements strictly, or an accidental error. For this reason, bugs must often be described superficially, without reference to underlying cause.

5. Finding the Best Interpretation

The previous sections have described how PROUST generates interpretations for programs. However, PROUST must not only construct interpretations, it must select from among rival interpretations. As we saw in Section 3.3, when PROUST constructs goal decompositions for a program, it constructs a tree of alternative goal decompositions. After the plans are matched, PROUST decides which goal decompositions to explore further. Actually, that is not quite correct; the choice of goal decomposition depends not only upon which plans match, but also how the mismatches are explained in terms of bugs. PROUST is thus comparing program interpretations, not just plan matches. This section describes how PROUST attempts to arrive at the best available interpretation for each program.

Three things are required in order to make sure that PROUST finds the best possible interpretation. First, goals must be selected for decomposition in an order such that interpretation choices are not simply the result of ambiguous plan matches; the methods for selecting goals were described earlier in Section 3.4. Second, evaluation criteria are needed to make sure that each interpretation makes sense. Third, heuristics are required for comparing different interpretations. The discussion in this section will focus on the latter two issues.

5.1. An example of selection among interpretations

In order to show how alternative interpretations for programs can arise, let us return to the example of the Rainfall Problem that was introduced in Fig. 1. The loop from this example is repeated in Fig. 16. One goal decomposition for this loop was discussed in Section 3.1. Now let us consider an alternative goal decomposition for *Sentinel-Controlled Input Sequence*, and see how the program interpretations based upon these two goal decompositions can be compared.

Recall that PROUST knows about four different plans for implementing the goal *Sentinel-Controlled Input Sequence*. Up to now the discussion has focused on one of these plans, the SENTINEL READ-PROCESS REPEAT PLAN. Now let us consider what happens when one of the other plans, the SENTINEL PROCESS-READ WHILE PLAN, is matched against the program. This plan is shown in Fig. 17. In this plan, the first value is input before the main loop is entered; this

```
 8 repeat
 9    writeln ('Enter rainfall');
10    readln;
11    read (Rain);
12    while Rain < 0 do
13      begin
14        Writeln (Rain:0:2, 'is not possible, try again');
15        readln;
16        read (Rain)
17      end;
18
19    while Rain <> 99999 do
20      begin
21        if Rain = 0 then
22           Drydays := Drydays + 1;
23        Totalrain := Totalrain + Rain;
24        if Rain > 0 then
25           Raindays := Raindays + 1;
26        if Highrain < Rain then
27           Highrain := Rain
28      end;
29 until Rain = 99999;
```

Fig. 16. The loop in the example in Fig. 1.

input serves to initialize the variable ?New. The loop itself uses a while statement instead of a repeat statement. The Next step of the loop, which reads in the successive values of ?New, is at the bottom of the loop, instead of at the top, unlike the SENTINEL READ-PROCESS REPEAT PLAN. The part of the loop where the data is processed, labeled Process, is above the Next step. Because the processing step is above the next input step in the loop, no additional *Sentinel Guard* subgoal is required to break out of the loop. In what follows, the SENTINEL PROCESS-READ WHILE PLAN will be abbreviated as S P-R W PLAN, and the SENTINEL READ-PROCESS REPEAT PLAN will be abbreviated as S R-P R PLAN.

The S P-R W PLAN can match the program at least partially, since the program

SENTINEL PROCESS-READ WHILE PLAN

Constants: ?Stop
Variables: ?New
Template:
　Initinput:　*subgoal Input(?New)*
　Mainloop:　while (?New <> ?Stop) do
　　　　　　　　begin
　Process:　　　? *
　Next:　　　　*subgoal Input(?New)*
　　　　　　　　end

Fig. 17. Another plan for inplementing *Sentinel-Controlled Input Sequence*.

has a while statement at line 19 which matches the while statement pattern in the plan. Using this plan as a starting point, an interpretation of the loop can be constructed. This interpretation is as follows.

> The while statement in the S P-R W PLAN matches line 19 in the program. The begin-end pair matches lines 20 and 28. The initial *Input* subgoal is combined with the *Input Validation* goal in the problem description, yielding the composite goal *Validated Input*. The VALIDATED PROCESS-READ WHILE INPUT PLAN is a possible implementation of this goal, and it matches lines 10 through 17. The *Input* subgoal in the Next step of the S P-R W PLAN cannot be matched against the program. The student must have omitted implementation of this subgoal. The probable cause is a misconception about iterative inputs; the student may have thought that successive input values would be read in automatically.

The principal differences between the interpretation based upon the S R-P R PLAN and the one based upon the S P-R W PLAN are as follows. The S R-P R PLAN interpretation makes the repeat loop at line 8 the main loop; the S P-R W PLAN makes the while loop at line 19 the main loop. The S R-P R PLAN interpretation regards the input and validation code at lines 10 through 17 as a Next step in the loop; the other interpretation views it as an initialization step. The S P-R W PLAN interpretation gives no interpretation whatsoever to the repeat loop. The S P-R W PLAN interpretation has a missing-input bug, whereas the other interpretation has a while-for-if bug.

Of the various differences mentioned above, the key ones are that the S R-P R PLAN matches more of the program, and does not have any plan components missing. PROUST has an interpretation evaluation heuristic that is relevant to this case:

> Avoid interpretations that leave significant parts of the program uninterpreted.

The rationale for this heuristic is as follows. Each statement is presumed to have a purpose, so if no purpose can be found for a statement, PROUST's goal decomposition may be incorrect. When one interpretation assigns a goal to every statement, and the other interpretation leaves statements without goals, the interpretation which leaves statements without goals is almost certainly incorrect.

The problem with the above evaluation heuristic is that it cannot be applied until the entire goal decomposition is constructed and matched against the program. If PROUST were unable to evaluate interpretations until after they are complete, it would construct large numbers of interpretations, only to find that nearly all of them are wrong. PROUST therefore applies the above heuristic only as a last resort. Instead, it applies other heuristics to detect bad interpretations before the analysis goes too far. The actual heuristic which is applied in this case is the following:

> Favor interpretations that match more of the program, and have
> fewer missing plan components.

If this heuristic is applied consistently, PROUST will usually end up with an interpretation which assigns a purpose to as many statements in the program as possible. The heuristic favors the SENTINEL PROCESS-READ REPEAT interpretation because it both matches more of the code and has no missing plan components.

This example illustrates the two kinds of interpretation evaluation processes in PROUST. One kind of evaluation compares one interpretation against other competing interpretations; this is called *differential evaluation* of interpretations. The other kind of evaluation examines the interpretation in isolation, usually after the interpretation is complete; this is called *interpretation assessment*. Both kinds of interpretation will be discussed below.

5.2. Differential evaluation of interpretations

Differentiating program interpretations is closely related to the notion of differential diagnosis in medicine. In performing differential diagnosis a physician compiles a set of etiologies, or causes, which might be relevant to the patient's symptoms. This set of etiologies is called a differential. The physician then tries to narrow down the differential by comparing etiologies against each other, and looking for evidence which confirms one subset of etiologies and disconfirms the others. Eventually the differential is narrowed down to a single diagnosis, the diagnosis which wins out at the end will be demonstrably superior to the alternatives. If, on the other hand, the diagnostician cannot distinguish between competing etiologies, the diagnosis must be considered inconclusive.

The intention-based approach to program analysis lends itself naturally to differential diagnosis. When a goal is selected for analysis, different implementations of the goal are suggested. The set of candidate implementations forms a differential. PROUST then decides which among these implementations fits the program best. Differentiation leads to more robust bug analysis because it allows PROUST to find a wide range of uncommon bugs, bugs which out of context could not be assumed to be present. For example, the while-for-if bugs are hard to identify out of context. Most novice programmers understand the difference between while and if, so PROUST could not presume a while-if confusion without independent evidence. If the while-for-if bug is part of an interpretation that is better than any other interpretation, then the while-for-if diagnosis can be given with more confidence.

Although differential evaluation is desirable, generation of numerous alternative interpretations is undesirable, as it will slow the system down. There are two ways to get around this problem.

- Differentially evaluate partial interpretations.
- Generate just one interpretation; then when the interpretation is complete, perform the differential evaluation, and change the interpretation to reflect the result of the differential evaluation.

The former approach was used in the while-for-if example to determine which plan is used to implement the *Sentinel-Controlled Input Sequence* goal. The latter approach is commonly used in determining whether misconceptions are present. For example, suppose that PROUST finds that an initialization is missing. It can either describe the missing initialization as an accidental bug, or as a manifestation of a misconception about initializations. The two interpretations can be differentiated by checking whether or not initializations were systematically omitted; but such a check cannot be performed until after the interpretation is completed. What PROUST does in this case is to describe the missing initialization independent of cause, and wait until after the interpretation is complete to decide what the cause is likely to be. If it turns out that the initialization bug is systematic, then the bug descriptions of all the missing initializations are changed to indicate a possible misconception.

Differential evaluation of complete interpretations is straightforward, since a substantial amount of information is available for use in comparing interpretations. For example, once the entire program is analyzed, PROUST can check whether or not goals were assigned to every part of the program. Differential evaluation of partial interpretations, on the other hand, is much trickier. The differential interpretation in the previous section is a case in point. When PROUST tries to designate the while statement as the main loop, it is leaving the repeat statement uninterpreted. At this point it is not known whether or not there is some other goal pending on the goal agenda that might account for repeat statement. PROUST is thus making the differentiation on the basis of incomplete information, and must rely upon heuristic comparisons of the partial interpretations. The following discussion will focus on differential evaluation of partial interpretations, and show why PROUST's heuristic approach is usually successful.

5.2.1. *Differential evaluation of partial interpretations*

Differential evaluation of partial interpretations is performed at each branch point in the interpretation tree where plans are selected. As described earlier, whenever a goal is selected for decomposition a number of branches of the tree are constructed, each branch ending in a plan. The plans are then matched in parallel. If some of the plans have mismatches, plan-difference rules are applied to explain the mismatches. If a mismatch cannot be explained, the offending plan component is presumed to be missing from the program. Once plan matching and plan-difference analysis is complete, the differential evaluation process can begin.

The first step in choosing among plans is to filter out those which have implausibly many components missing. We consider it plausible that a component be missing if in our empirical studies of novice programs we observe that novice programmers occasionally leave the component out. For example, it is plausible for the initialization component of any plan to be missing. There exists a set of rules in PROUST's knowledge base, similar to plan-difference rules, which trigger when plan components are found to be missing, and indicate what bugs might cause them. If no rules can account for why a plan has missing components, the plan is thrown out.[4] All that remain are plans that can be mapped onto the code in some plausible way. If all plans for a given goal are thrown out, then PROUST concludes that the program does not implement the goal.

The second step in choosing a plan is to count the number of components that matched in each plan, and select those with the greatest number of matched components. In other words, PROUST selects the greediest match. It is this criterion which determines that the repeat loop is the main loop in the program in Fig. 16. Greedy selection works for two reasons. First, not many large plans pass the first selection step; those which remain are probably the right matches. Second, if greedy selection picks the wrong plan, the selection error will probably be discovered later, when a plan implementing a different goal is found to match the same code. When two plans implementing different goals match the same code, one or the other of the two plans is likely to be matched incorrectly. Our ultimate aim is to give PROUST the capability of then deciding between the two matches to the same code, and choosing different plans to remove the conflict.

If two plans have the same number of matching components, they are further differentiated by counting the number of misconceptions that are suggested by the plan-difference rules. Interpretations which do not suggest misconceptions are favored over those which do.

If these criteria fail to identify a unique interpretation as the best match, PROUST puts the analysis of the goal aside, and selects a different goal for decomposition. PROUST will then reconsider the analysis of the goal later, after other goals have been analyzed. This allows PROUST to rely upon Occam's razor in selecting interpretations. PROUST assumes that each part of the program serves a unique purpose, unless the goal decomposition explicitly dictates that two goals are being combined. If part of the program clearly implements a particular goal, then it can be assumed that it does not match any other goals. Interpretations of the other goals are restricted to those parts of the program which have not previously been interpreted. The following

---

[4] These missing-component rules were first introduced before PROUST's differential evaluation mechanism was in place. It now appears that these rules can be replaced by more general heuristics that can be incorporated into the differential evaluation mechanism.

example serves to illustrate. Suppose that a student confuses running total updates and counter updates, writing Sum := Sum + 1 instead of Sum := Sum + New. In such cases it may be hard to tell which update is supposed to be the running total update, since there may be several increment statements in the program. If PROUST postpones the decision and matches the *Count* goals instead, then through a process of elimination PROUST can eventually identify the buggy running total update.

5.3. Interpretation assessment

In spite of PROUST's attempts to select the best interpretation for programs, it sometimes makes mistakes. Programs sometimes have bugs that PROUST's plan-difference rules cannot recognize. The programmer may use variables in inconsistent ways, giving PROUST false expectations about the bindings of pattern variables in plans. In order to make sure that no mistake was made in interpreting the program, PROUST examines the program interpretation as a whole once analysis is complete, looking for evidence that the interpretation is incorrect. If such evidence is found, questionable parts of the interpretation are deleted, to guard against giving an incorrect bug report to the student.

The most obvious indication of interpretation failure is that very few of the goals in the problem description were successfully mapped onto the student's code. PROUST requires that interpretations be found for a significant fraction of the goals in the problem description. If this fails to happen, the analysis is aborted, and no bugs are reported to the student.

Even if most of the goals are mapped onto the code, the analysis is possibly flawed if some of the code could not be analyzed, and some of the goals could not be mapped onto the code. When this happens, PROUST performs bottom-up analysis on the interpreted code, to see what kind of function it performs, and then compares this against the outstanding goals. If the function of some of the code is close to one or more of the outstanding goals, then the interpretation is probably in error. The interpretation is classified by PROUST as a partial analysis. Bugs which may be in error because of the misinterpretation, such as complaints about unimplemented goals, are deleted from the bug report that is presented to the student. This process is described in more detail in [16].

6. Empirical Evaluation of PROUST

The bottom-line issue in evaluating the work that has gone into PROUST is whether or not it has resulted in an effective tool for finding novice bugs. This cannot be determined by observing PROUST's behavior on a few student programs; instead, PROUST must be tested on hundreds of student programs, in a variety of situations. The results of some of these empirical tests are presented below. Further results are published elsewhere [16].

6.1. Results on the Rainfall Problem

Table 1 shows the results of running PROUST off-line on a corpus of 206 different solutions of the Rainfall Problem. The percentage of programs which are analyzed completely is 81%. PROUST's analysis is complete if a complete interpretation was generated, in which interpretation assessment could not find any inconsistencies. 15% of the programs were analyzed partially, meaning that a substantial part of the program was analyzed, but the interpretation was incomplete or inconsistent. In 4% of the cases the analysis was aborted, either because hardly any goals were successfully analyzed or because some construct such as goto, which PROUST is not prepared to analyze, appears in the program. When PROUST analyzes programs completely, it identifies 94% of the bugs, as determined by hand analyses of the same programs. Note that these were not 94% of the bugs that we expected PROUST to detect; they were 94% of *all semantic and logical errors*. At the same time there are a certain number of false alarms, i.e., cases where PROUST either misinterpreted a bug or flagged a bug which did not really exist. Most of these false alarms result from misinterpretations of the programs' goal decompositions, often because an unusual plan or bug was present. Further extension and generalization of PROUST's knowledge base would be required in order to reduce the occurrence of false alarms. The Rainfall Problem was subsequently assigned to another PASCAL class, and was tested on line. The subsequent results were comparable, with 70% of the programs receiving full analysis, and 98% of the bugs in these programs correctly recognized.

Table 1
Results of running PROUST on the Rainfall Problem

Total number of programs:	206	
Number of programs with bugs:	183	(89%)
Number of programs without bugs:	23	
Total number of bugs:	795	
Number of programs receiving full analyses:	167	(81%)
Total number of bugs:	598	(75%)
Bugs recognized correctly:	562	(94%)
Bugs not recognized:	36	(6%)
False alarms:	66	
Number of programs receiving partial analyses:	31	(15%)
Total number of bugs:	167	(21%)
Bugs recognized correctly:	61	(37%)
Bugs not reported:	106	(63%)
False alarms:	20	
Number of programs PROUST did not analyze:	9	(4%)
Total number of bugs:	32	(4%)

6.1.1. *Results on a different problem*

In a further test, PROUST was tested on a different programming problem, called the Bank Problem.

Bank Problem. Write a PASCAL program that processes three types of bank transactions: withdrawals, deposits, and a special transaction that says: no more transactions are to follow. Your program should start by asking the user to input his/her account id and his/her initial balance. Then your program should prompt the user to input
(1) the transaction type,
(2) if it is an END-PROCESSING transaction, the program should print out (a) the final balance of the user's account, (b) the total number of transactions, (c) the total number of each type of transaction, and (d) the total amount of the service charges, and stop;
(3) if it is a DEPOSIT or a WITHDRAWAL, the program should ask for the amount of the transaction and then post it appropriately.
Use a variable of type CHAR to encode the transaction types. To encourage saving, charge the user 20 cents per withdrawal, but nothing for a deposit.

In this problem, the students are required to write a program which behaves similarly to an automatic bank teller machine. The program is supposed to input a series of deposit and withdrawal commands, followed by an end-processing command. The user's account balance is updated according to the amount of each deposit and withdrawal. At the end of the program a summary of the transactions is printed.

Table 2 shows PROUST's current performance on the Bank Problem. The frequency of completed analyses is much lower than in the case of the Rainfall Problem; it analyzed 50% of the programs, as opposed to 81% on the Rainfall Problem. PROUST's performance on the completely analyzed programs is almost as good as it is on completely analyzed solutions of the Rainfall Problem. 91% of the bugs in the Bank Problem solutions were correctly identified, compared with 94% of the bugs in the Rainfall Problem solutions. The incidence of false alarms, however, is relatively high; there were 41 false alarms in the completely analyzed Bank Problem solutions, compared with 211 total bugs in the same group of programs. Four programs were omitted from analysis because they were very far removed from an expected solution, to such an extent that they were not considered a fair test of PROUST.

There appear to be several reasons why PROUST's performance on the Bank Problem is less than that on the Rainfall Problem. First, the problem requires that more goals be satisfied than the Rainfall Problem requires; this was an intended feature of the problem. Other problems with the Bank Problem, however, were unanticipated. For one thing, many more of the goals of the Bank Problem were left implicit. For example, the problem statement says

Table 2
Results of running PROUST on the Bank Problem

Total number of programs analyzed:	64	
Total numbers of bugs	420	
Number of programs receiving full analyses:	32	(50%)
Total number of bugs:	211	(50%)
Bugs recognized correctly:	191	(91%)
Bugs not reported:	20	(9%)
False alarms:	41	
Number of programs receiving partial analyses:	26	(41%)
Total number of bugs:	168	(40%)
Bugs recognized correctly:	56	(33%)
Bugs not reported:	112	(67%)
False alarms:	24	
Number of programs PROUST did not analyze:	6	(9%)
Total number of bugs:	41	(10%)
Number of programs omitted from analysis:	4	

nothing about what to do if the balance becomes less than zero. Some solutions had no checks for negative balance, some checked the balance only after the last transaction is complete, and some checked the balance after each transaction. PROUST did not generate all of these different goal decompositions, so it failed to interpret some programs. Another difference between the two problems is that the Bank Problem provides no explicit cues to disambiguate plan matching. The Rainfall Problem states explicitly that the sentinel value is 99999; the plans for matching *Sentinel-Controlled Input Sequence* therefore usually match unambiguously, since there is only one loop in a given solution which tests for 99999. The Bank Problem, on the other hand, does not state specifically which commands are to be used to indicate deposit, withdrawal, or end-processing transactions. There is therefore a much greater risk of ambiguous matches, and consequently of misinterpretations of the program. It appears likely that a more detailed problem statement, in which the transaction commands were listed explicitly, would have improved PROUST's performance.

7. Concluding Remarks and Future Directions

This article has claimed that accurate debugging of novice programs requires an understanding of the intentions underlying programs. Without an understanding of the programmer's intentions, many bugs cannot be detected, and those that can be detected cannot be localized and explained. In order to diagnose bugs effectively, one needs knowledge both of what the program is intended to do and how it is intended to do it. Since the intentions underlying each program may be different, the precise intentions of the programmer must be inferred from the buggy program as it is being analyzed. The key to doing this is to start with a description of the problem being solved, and to use programming knowledge to predict possible ways in which the problem might be solved. In most cases the programmer's intentions can be related to the predictions. A program called PROUST was built which uses this approach to diagnose bugs in novice programs.

Although significant results have been achieved so far with PROUST, much more work remains to be done. One of the most immediate needs at this time is to test PROUST on a wider range of programming problems. Now that an acceptable level of performance has been achieved on two programming problems, the time has come to try to generalize and extend PROUST's knowledge. In addition, detailed feedback from novice users would be helpful, to ensure that PROUST's goal decompositions accurately reflect the novices' intentions.

Until PROUST is coupled with a tutoring module, PROUST's ability to diagnose programming errors will remain limited to the information that is extractable from the buggy programs themselves. A tutoring component would be able to ask students questions in order to select between alternative explanations of bugs. It would allow PROUST to refine its model of the student's abilities, to make more explicit its model of the student's knowledge and problem-solving skills. This in turn would allow PROUST to make more accurate predictions about the students' intentions, and derive a deeper understanding of the students' bugs. Such a tutor is currently in the process of being developed [20, 22].

A version of PROUST should be developed for a different programming language, such as ADA or LISP. Building such a system would help determine the generality of PROUST's approach, and would provide further insights into the kinds of knowledge that programmers use in solving problems. It would also be useful to apply PROUST's approach to other domains, in order to demonstrate the generality of intention-based analysis as a means for identifying and correcting bugs. There are already some promising results in this direction: Sebrechts has taken a stripped-down version of PROUST, called MICRO-PROUST [18], and adapted it to the domain of statistics. The resulting system, GIDE, has undergone preliminary tests with statistics students [24]. PROUST's approach should be useful in a variety of domains where students are given sets of goals to solve, and must combine plans in order to construct a solution which achieves these goals.

ACKNOWLEDGMENT

I would like to thank Elliot Soloway, my advisor, for insightful suggestions regarding this research, and for comments on an earlier draft of this paper. I would also like to thank Bill Clancey for his comments regarding this paper, and for his help in clarifying some of the ideas presented here. Bill Swartout and Bob Neches also made helpful suggestions regarding the paper.

This work was co-sponsored by the Personnel and Training Research Groups, Psychological Sciences Division, Office of Naval Research and the Army Research Institute for the Behavioral and Social Sciences, under Contract No. N00014-82-K-0714, Contract Authority Identification Number, No. 154-492. Approved for public release; distribution unlimited. Reproduction in whole or part is permitted for any purpose of the United States Government.

REFERENCES

1. Adam, A. and Laurent, J.-P., LAURA: A system to debug student programs, *Artificial Intelligence* **15** (1980) 75–122.
2. Barnard, D.T., A survey of syntax error handling techniques, Tech. Rept., University of Toronto, Toronto, Ont. (1976).
3. Bonar, J., Ehrlich, K. and Soloway, E., Collecting and analyzing on-line protocols from novice programmers, *Behav. Res. Methods Instrumentation* **14** (1982) 203–209.
4. Brown, J.S. and Burton, R.R., Diagnostic models for procedural bugs in mathematics, *Cognitive Sci.* **2** (1978) 155–192.
5. Burton, R.R., Diagnosing bugs in a simple procedural skill, in: D. Sleeman and J.S. Brown (Eds.), *Intelligent Tutoring Systems* (Academic Press, New York, 1982).
6. Conway, R.W. and Wilcox, T.R., Design and implementation of a diagnostic compiler for PL/I, *Commun. ACM* **16** (1973) 169–179.
7. Davis, R., Shrobe, H., Hamscher, W., Weickert, K., Shirley, M. and Polit, S., Diagnosis based on description of structure and function, in: *Proceedings AAAI-82*, Pittsburgh, PA (1982) 137–142.
8. Eisenstadt, M., Prospective zooming: A knowledge based tracing and debugging methodology for logic programming, in: *Proceedings IJCAI-85*, Los Angeles, CA (1985) 717–719.
9. Farrell, R.G., Anderson, J.R. and Reiser, B.J., An interactive computer-based tutor for LISP, in: *Proceedings AAAI-84*, Austin, TX (1984) 106–109.
10. Fosdick, L.D. and Osterweil, L.J., Data flow analysis in software reliability, *Comput. Surv.* **8** (1976) 305–330.
11. Genesereth, M.R., Automated consultation for complex computer systems, Ph.D. Thesis, Harvard University, Cambridge, MA (1978).
12. Genesereth, M.R., The role of plans in intelligent teaching systems, in: D. Sleeman and J.S. Brown (Eds.), *Intelligent Tutoring Systems* (Academic Press, New York, 1982).
13. Graham, S.L. and Rhodes, S.P., Practical syntactic error recovery in compilers, *Commun. ACM* **18** (11) (1975).
14. Harandi, M.T., Knowledge-based program debugging: A heuristic model, in: *Proceedings 1983 SOFTFAIR* (1983).
15. James, E.B. and Partridge, D.P., Adaptive correction of program statements, *Commun. ACM* **16** (1) (1973).
16. Johnson, W.L., *Intention-Based Diagnosis of Novice Programming Errors* (Morgan Kaufmann, Los Altos, CA, 1986).
17. Johnson, W.L., Draper, S. and Soloway, E., Classifying bugs is a tricky business, in: *Proceedings NASA Workshop on Software Engineering* (to appear).
18. Johnson, W.L. and Soloway, E., PROUST: An automatic debugger for Pascal programs, in: *Artificial Intelligence and Instruction: Applications and Methods* (Addison-Wesley, Reading, MA, 1986).
19. Johnson, W.L., Soloway, E., Cutler, B. and Draper, S., Bug collection I, Tech. Rept. 296, Department of Computer Science, Yale University, New Haven, CT (1983).
20. Littman, D.C., Pinto, J. and Soloway, E., An analysis of tutorial reasoning about programming bugs, in: *Proceedings AAAI-86*, Philadelphia, PA (1986) 320–326.
21. Murray, W.R., Automatic program debugging for intelligent tutoring systems, Ph.D. Thesis, University of Texas, Austin, TX (1986).

22. Rich, C., A formal representation for plans in the programmer's apprentice, in: *Proceedings IJCAI-81*, Vancouver, BC (1981) 1044–1052.
23. Sack, W. and Soloway, E., From MENO to PROUST to CHIRON: AI design as iterative engineering; Intermediate results are important!, in: *Proceedings Invited Workshop on Computer-Based Learning Environments*, Pittsburgh, PA (1988).
24. Sebrechts, M., Schooler, L., LaClaire, L. and Soloway, E., Computer-based interpretations of students' statistical errors: A preliminary empirical analysis of GIDE, in: *Proceedings 8th National Educational Computing Conference*, Philadelphia, PA (1987).
25. Sedlmeyer, R.L. and Johnson, P.E., Diagnostic reasoning in software fault localization, in: *Proceedings SIGSOFT Workshop on High-Level Debugging*, Asilomar, CA (1983).
26. Shapiro, D.G., Sniffer: A system that understands bugs, Tech. Rept. AI Memo 638, MIT Artificial Intelligence Laboratory, Cambridge, MA (1981).
27. Shapiro, E., *Algorithmic Program Debugging* (MIT Press, Cambridge, MA, 1982).
28. Sleeman, D., A rule directed modelling system, in: R.S. Michalski, J.G. Carbonell and T.M. Mitchell (Eds.), *Machine Learning: An Artificial Intelligent Approach* (Tioga, Palo Alto, CA, 1983).
29. Soloway, E. and Ehrlich, K., Empirical investigations of programming knowledge, *IEEE Trans. Software Eng.* **10** (5) (1984).
30. Soloway, E., Rubin, E., Woolf, B., Bonar, J. and Johnson, W.L., MENO-II: An AI-based programming-tutor, *J. Comput.-Based Instruction* **10** (1) (1983).
31. Swartout, W., The Gist behavior explainer, in: *Proceedings AAAI-83*, Washington, DC (1983). (Also available as ISI/RR-83-3.)
32. Teitelman, W., *INTERLISP Reference Manual* (1978).
33. Wertz, H., Stereotyped program debugging: An aid for novice programmers, *Int. J. Man-Mach. Stud.* **16** (1982) 379–392.

.

Causal Model Progressions as a Foundation for Intelligent Learning Environments

Barbara Y. White and John R. Frederiksen

BBN Laboratories, 10 Moulton Street, Cambridge, MA 02138, USA

ABSTRACT

AI research in qualitative modeling makes possible new approaches to teaching people about science and technology. We are exploring the implications of this work for the design of intelligent learning environments. The domain of application is electrical circuits, but the approach can be generalized to other subjects. Our prototype instructional system is based upon a progression of qualitative models of electrical circuit behavior. These models enable the system to simulate circuit behavior and to generate causal explanations. They also serve as target mental models for the learner. The model progression is used to create problem sets that motivate successive refinements to the students' mental models. Acquisition of these models allows students, at all stages of learning, to solve interesting problems, such as circuit design and troubleshooting problems. The system enables students to employ different learning strategies and to manage their own learning. For instance, they can create and experiment with circuits, can attempt problems posed by the system, and can ask for feedback and coaching from the models. In pilot trials, the learning environment successfully taught novices to troubleshoot and to mentally simulate circuit behavior.

1. Introduction

Our objective has been to create a powerful intelligent learning environment that enables students to utilize a wide range of learning strategies as they seek to develop expertise within a domain. We wanted to develop a system that would support not only learning from explanations, but also learning by discovery. The domain of instruction we selected is electrical circuits and the laws that govern their behavior. However, the architecture of the learning environment could readily be generalized to other domains.

To create the intelligent learning environment, we designed a progression of qualitative, causal models of electrical circuit behavior that represent a transition from naivete to expertise. These qualitative models serve to drive circuit simulations, and to generate causal explanations of circuit behavior. They are implemented within the instructional system as a set of "articulate models"

Artificial Intelligence **42** (1990) 99–157

that can visually simulate and verbally explain what happens in a circuit when, for example, a switch is closed. When students interact with the computer, they are playing a "guess my model" game in that they are attempting to induce the computer's current model. After they have assimilated a given model, students move on to the next, more sophisticated, model in the sequence. Each such model progression is used to define a problem set that fosters that particular refinement in the student's mental model.[1] The central feature of the approach is that, at each stage of learning, the model driving the computer simulation represents the mental model that the student is to acquire.

This new type of instructional environment synthesizes features of intelligent tutoring systems with features of microworlds. As a microworld, it provides for open-ended exploration within an interactive simulation that enables one to discover its laws. As a tutoring environment, it provides facilities for generating explanations, for modelling how to solve problems, for sequencing problems based upon the student's evolving mental model, and for providing intelligent feedback.

While the prototype system described in this article is restricted to helping students understand the behavior of electrical circuits, the approach can be applied to a large number of domains. For instance, any domain whose phenomena can be represented by laws affecting the behavior of objects can potentially be tutored using causal model progressions. This includes physical systems (e.g., Newtonian mechanics [50]), biological systems (e.g., the human heart [18]), or even economic systems. Causal modeling can also be applied to the learning of mathematical systems—as in the work of Feurzeig and White [20] that used an articulate causal model to help elementary school students understand place notation and its relationship to the standard algorithms for addition and subtraction. Further, this approach could be applied to learning about computers themselves: articulate causal models could help students understand, design, and troubleshoot computer hardware and software (such as when attempting to debug a computer program or to understand how a compiler works). Thus, we argue that causal model progressions have broad applicability as a foundation for intelligent learning environments.

1.1. Mental models

The theoretical framework we adopt is that expertise (in this case, electrical expertise) can be captured by a small set of mental models that embody alternative, but coordinated, conceptualizations of system operation. For in-

---

[1] By mental model we mean a knowledge structure that incorporates both declarative knowledge (e.g., device models) and procedural knowledge (e.g., procedures for determining distributions of voltages within a circuit), and a control structure that determines how the procedural and declarative knowledge are used in solving problems (e.g., mentally simulating the behavior of a circuit).

stance, experts utilize qualitative as well as quantitative models, and behavioral as well as functional models. We adopt this viewpoint based upon both empirical and theoretical research. Our models are derived from extensive studies of an expert troubleshooter who teaches in a technical high school [45, 46]. The models that we present to students are also influenced by studies of students' reasoning about circuit problems (e.g., [9, 10]), and also draw upon theoretical AI work on qualitative modeling [12, 14, 16, 21, 32, 43, 51], particularly that of de Kleer and Brown [15].

We chose mental models as the knowledge structures that we would try to impart to students for several reasons. First, it is our belief that students learn most effectively when they are actively applying their knowledge to solving problems. To support such learning-by-problem-solving, students must, at all times, maintain a knowledge structure that is complete enough to support problem solving. Thus, the purpose of the intelligent learning environment is to develop in students a progression of increasingly sophisticated mental models for reasoning about circuit behavior, each capable of supporting problem solving for a subset of circuit problems.

Second, as de Kleer and Brown [16] have argued, such models can embody concepts and laws, can generate causal accounts, and can enable problem solving in a wide range of contexts. For example, the same mental model can be used for making predictions about the behavior of different circuits, for troubleshooting circuits, and for designing circuits. This is in contrast with, for example, troubleshooting knowledge represented as symptom-fault associations, which are context-specific and not explicitly causal, and are, therefore, of limited use in helping students to understand how circuits work.

In addition to being efficient and powerful knowledge structures for students to possess, mental models are also efficient and powerful knowledge structures upon which to base an intelligent learning environment. At any given point in the student's knowledge evolution, a single model can provide not only a model of how one wants the student to reason, but also can provide an interactive simulation of domain phenomena. This simulation is capable, by simply reasoning out loud (via a speech synthesis device), of generating causal accounts for the behavior of a circuit that the student is creating and observing. For instance, the student can close a switch and see a light turn on and, at the same time, hear an explanation of how changes in the conductivity of the switch caused a change in the voltage applied to the light, which in turn caused the light to turn on. Thus, we argue that mental models can, if appropriately designed, enable both the instructional system and the student to reason from general principles and to generate causal accounts of circuit behavior.

We will argue that these models should initially be qualitative and able to generate causal accounts of the changes in devices' states that occur during the operation of a circuit. Thus, they should be capable of reasoning about device states and about the processes that lead to changes in those states. In addition, we claim that the form of qualitative models employed should facilitate learning alternative conceptualizations of how circuits work. The concepts and reasoning processes employed in qualitative models should, for example, be compatible with quantitative models of circuit behavior, with reductionistic, physical models of electricity, and with functional accounts of system operation. This is important not only for facilitating the learning of multiple conceptualizations, but also for reasoning using multiple conceptualizations in the course of solving problems.

1.1.1. *The importance of qualitative reasoning*

When novices and experts reason about physical domains, their approach to solving problems has something in common: Both employ primarily qualitative reasoning. Experts reason qualitatively about the phenomena before they resort to quantitative formalizations [7, 33], whereas novices are only capable of qualitative, and often incorrect, reasoning. If, however, one looks at less naive novices, such as people who have had one or two years of physics instruction, their reasoning is primarily quantitative and involves searching for equations that contain the givens in the problem [7, 33]. This discrepancy is due, in part, to the emphasis placed, in most physics instruction, on learning quantitative methods and on solving quantitative problems. Experts, like beginning novices, make extensive use of qualitative reasoning. In the domain of electricity, for example, de Kleer observes that, "an engineer does not perform a quantitative analysis unless he first understands the circuit at a qualitative level." [14, p. 275].

We therefore argue that students should initially be exposed to qualitative, causal reasoning in order (1) to make connections with their naive intuitive models of physical phenomena [17], and (2) to enable them to acquire this important problem-solving skill that evidence has shown they lack [7, 33]. Quantitative reasoning should only be introduced after students have been given a qualitative, causal conception of the domain, and the form of quantitative reasoning then taught should be a logical extension of the qualitative reasoning they have acquired. Further, the form of qualitative, causal reasoning should build upon students' naive but accurate intuitions and thus help to override their inaccurate intuitions. In this regard, it should be compatible with reasoning employed in other physical domains, such as mechanics, about which students' may have knowledge and experience that can be drawn upon during learning. It should also be compatible with students' intuitions about the causal nature of the world, such as: "changes in states have precipitating causes."

This initial emphasis on qualitative thinking requires that students be given problems that necessitate qualitative, causal reasoning for their solution. For instance, in the domain of electrical circuits, problems involving the prediction of circuit behavior, circuit design, and troubleshooting all have this property. Problems of this type are thus useful in motivating the development of qualitative reasoning skills.

1.1.2. *Causal consistency*

Conventionally, electrical theory is taught by presenting a series of laws which describe fundamental relations among voltage, current, and resistance in a circuit (e.g., Ohm's Law, and Kirchhoff's Voltage and Current Laws). The laws are presented as algebraic equations, which can be manipulated in their form (e.g., $I = V/R$, $V = IR$, $R = V/I$). Instruction then focuses on how to apply these equations in their various forms in order to analyze problems involving circuits of varying degrees of complexity. In these problems, the resulting constraints on voltages and currents in a circuit are used to develop quantitative solutions for the unknown quantities in the problem. Note that by using such constraint-based reasoning, no explicit causal model is presented, and the implicit causal model is actually inconsistent. Thus, at times the current flowing through a fixed resistance is viewed as determining the voltage, and at other times applied voltages are viewed as determining the current through a resistance. In addition, the order in which the constraint equations are applied when solving problems is governed by algebraic considerations rather than by a causal analysis. Thus the problem-solving process that students are taught does not necessarily facilitate an understanding of the physical system under study.

It is also the case that qualitative theories are not necessarily consistent about the basic causal relations between voltage, current, and resistance. For example, de Kleer's EQUAL [14] infers that an increase in current out of a node causes a decrease in the voltage at that node (using what he terms the KCL heuristic). At other times, an increase in voltage across a component causes the current through the component to increase (using a qualitative version of Ohm's Law). Thus, the qualitative reasoning makes inferences about the effects of changes in current on voltage, and it also allows inferences about the effects of changes in voltage on current flow.

Our view is that mental models should be consistent in the assumed direction of causality among resistance, voltage, and current. In particular, current through a component is determined by the voltage or electric force applied to the component. Voltages applied to a component within a circuit are, in turn, determined by the input voltage and by resistances within the circuit. Viewing electric force as causing current flow also allows one to explain electrical phenomena that cannot be explained by current flow alone (for example, the behavior of capacitors; see [42]). Furthermore, this view is consistent with students' models of mechanics, in which forces applied in a particular direction accelerate a moving body. Finally, Cohen, Eylon and Ganiel [9] argue that this is an important way of conceptualizing circuit behavior that even sophisticated students lack, as illustrated by the following quotation:

> Current is the primary concept used by students, whereas potential difference is regarded as a *consequence* of current flow, and not as its *cause*. Consequently students often use $V = IR$ incorrectly. A battery is regarded as a source of constant current. The concepts of

emf and internal resistance are not well understood. Students have difficulties in analyzing the effect which a change in one component has on the rest of the circuit. [9]

Qualitative reasoning should therefore be based initially upon a subset of the constraints available in quantitative circuit theory, chosen for their causal consistency. With electrical force viewed as the causal agent, to understand a circuit's behavior one needs to understand how changes in the conductivity (resistance) of circuit components alter the distribution of voltages within the circuit. Changes in the conductivities of circuit components are thus taken as the independent variables.

1.1.3. *An overview of the qualitative model*

Within the qualitative model embedded in our tutoring system, any change in conductivity of a circuit component invokes a voltage redistribution process. This process determines the voltages that occur throughout the circuit as a result of such a change in conductivity. Qualitative rules that govern this voltage redistribution process are related to well-known laws of quantitative circuit theory (Kirchhoff's Voltage Law and Ohm's Law). They can also be seen as emergent properties of a dynamic model of the movement of charge carriers within a circuit as it settles into a steady state [24, 29]. Once the distribution of voltages is determined, the system then considers the effects of changes in voltage on the states of components within the circuit. For example, in a series circuit containing a switch, a light bulb, and a battery, if one closes the switch, the voltage across the switch becomes zero and that across the light bulb becomes nonzero. Then, since the light bulb has a voltage applied to it, it changes its state from "off" to "on." One can envision cases where the change in state of a component may also have an effect on its conductivity (such as when a transistor becomes saturated). This conductivity change in turn leads to another application of the voltage redistribution process, and so on. For example, if a switch is suddenly closed, it may cause a transistor to become saturated, which in turn could cause a light to go on. The sequence of propagation cycles continues until the circuit behavior stabilizes.

Simulating circuit behavior in this way, through the use of qualitative models, will reveal the sequence of device state changes that occur during the operation of the circuit and the reasons for those state changes. This allows the student to see how the behavior of devices is causally determined by changes in other devices' states, through the effects of those changes on the voltage distribution within the circuit. Understanding the causality of circuit behavior thus motivates the need to understand basic circuit concepts such as conductivity and voltage, and also basic circuit principles such as Kirchhoff's Voltage Law. These are nontrivial concepts and laws to master, so we have taken the approach of introducing them gradually, starting with simple circuits that can be reasoned about with simple forms of qualitative reasoning and progressing to more sophisticated circuits that require more sophisticated forms of qualitative reasoning for their analyses.

1.2. Learning as a process of model transformation

A view of learning that follows from the mental models approach is that, in the process of acquiring an expert model, the student formulates a series of models each of which is adequate for some subset of problems [46]. These models are transformed into increasingly more adequate models in response to the demands of more complex problems undertaken by the student. Thus, the primary learning construct is one of model transformation.

Transformations may involve the addition, modification, differentiation, or generalization of model features, or even the construction of alternative models. For example, students may learn to reason about discrete changes in states of devices on the basis of the voltages that are present within a circuit. Later, they may learn to reason about incremental changes in voltages and how they influence device states. These alternative models represent different ways of reasoning about a circuit, which share some concepts but differ in others. Other model transformations involve changes in a model's control structure. For instance, initially we focus on the behavior of a single device in a circuit, such as a light bulb, and how one reasons about the behavior of the light bulb as it is effected by changes in the circuit. Later in the model progression, we focus on how one reasons forward from a change in the circuit, such as closing a switch, to the effect on all of the devices within the circuit.

The representation of the learner's current knowledge state is a description of the set of models he or she currently has evolved [26]. This representation, in turn, characterizes the types of problems that the learner can currently solve. Our work has focused on creating *upward progressions* of increasingly sophisticated models for reasoning about the behavior of electrical circuits. We have also worked on *lateral progressions* that focus on alternative means for understanding circuit operation, such as models of circuit teleology and reductionistic, physical models of circuit behavior. All of these models furnish learning objectives for different stages in instruction.

For purposes of creating model progressions, we find it useful to define three dimensions on which models may vary: their *perspective*, their *order*, and their *degree of elaboration*. Lateral progressions, that represent alternative means of understanding the domain, involve changes in model perspective. Upward progressions to more sophisticated models involve changes in model order and degree of elaboration.

1.2.1. *The perspective of a model*

The "perspective" of a model refers to the nature of the model's reasoning in explaining a circuit's operation. For instance, it could be reasoning about:

(1) the high-level functionality of the circuit—e.g., its purpose and how subsystems within the circuit interact to achieve that purpose—i.e., *functional models*;

(2) the behavior of the circuit at the level of circuit components—e.g., how changes in the state of one device can cause changes in the states of other devices—i.e., *behavioral models*;

(3) the behavior of the circuit at a more micro level—e.g., how electrical charges are redistributed across a resistor when the voltage drop across the resistor changes—i.e., *reductionistic, physical models*.

In the first type of model, we represent devices as functional units that transmit and process information. The propagation mechanism involves information flow and takes into account functional dependencies among devices. In the second model, devices are represented as potential charge carriers (conductors) and sources of voltage, and the propagation mechanism utilizes qualitative, causal versions of basic circuit laws, such as Ohm's Law and Kirchhoff's Voltage Law, to reason about the electrical interactions among devices. In the third type of model, devices are represented at the molecular level in terms of their effects on the behavior of charge carriers, and the propagation mechanism is in terms of electrical forces and Coulomb's Law. Each of these models is qualitative and causal, yet each models a device from a different perspective, and propagates the effects of changes in device states by utilizing different laws (i.e., functional dependence versus Kirchhoff's Voltage Law versus Coulomb's Law). They are thus focusing on modeling different aspects of the domain phenomena.

1.2.2. *The order of a model*

In the context of the behavioral models, a further subdivision in this typology of models can be made. We distinguish models that reason on the basis of the mere *presence or absence* of resistance, voltage, or current, which we call "zero-order models," from those that reason on the basis of *incremental changes* in resistance, voltage, or current, which we call "first-order models." Zero-order models can reason about binary states of devices and can answer questions of the form, "Is there a voltage drop across the light in this circuit and, consequently, is the light off or on?" First-order models on the other hand reason on the basis of qualitative (first-order) derivatives and can answer questions such as, "Is there an increase in voltage across a component when we decrease the resistance of some other component?" Each of these is distinguished from quantitative models that can answer questions of the form, "What is the voltage across two points in a circuit?" All of these orders of model are thus useful for answering questions about circuit behavior of a particular sort.[2]

---

[2] Zero-order models, for example, are sometimes taught as a basis for learning to troubleshoot electrical circuits [45, 46].

For example, from the standpoint of the zero-order model, a simple one-transistor amplifier behaves like a switch, since the transistor has only two states: unsaturated (nonconductive) and saturated (conductive). Viewed within a first-order model, however, changes in the input voltage to the transistor cause incremental changes to the output voltage of the amplifier. This enables one to understand in qualitative terms the analogue behavior of the amplifier. From the viewpoint of a quantitative model, one can ascertain the range of input voltages for which this incremental behavior of the transistor remains true (that is, over what range of voltages the amplifier is linear). One could also synthesize zero- and first-order models by introducing the notion of boundary conditions on the input voltage to the transistor, in order to distinguish regions where the transistor follows the qualitative incremental model and those where it is fixed as unsaturated or saturated. The complexity of models which incorporate boundary conditions suggests that they should be reserved for problems in which such aspects of circuit behavior are important. Over the course of instruction, one seeks to develop an understanding of zero- and first-order models, and then such principles as boundary conditions which allow their integration. At the same time, students should develop a knowledge of the classes of problems for which each type of model is best suited.

1.2.3. *The degree of elaboration of a model*

During learning, qualitative models developed can increase in what we term their "degree of elaboration." This is determined by the number of qualitative rules used in propagating the effects of changes in states of circuit components on the behavior of other components. The qualitative rules employed are drawn from the repertoire of constraints of quantitative circuit theory, and initially focus on principles relating resistances to voltages within a circuit. These constraints are sufficient to understand and simulate the qualitative behavior of a large class of circuits, even though they are based upon only a subset of the available constraints of circuit theory (particularly, Kirchhoff's Voltage Law). In subsequent models, further qualitative rules are introduced (based on Ohm's Law and Kirchhoff's Current Law) to allow inferences about current flow within a circuit (as described in Section 3.3).

The purpose of presenting models of increasing degrees of constraint elaboration is to teach students to reason flexibly using the full set of constraints available to them, however redundant they may be for the purposes of qualitative reasoning about simple circuit behavior. This is important if one seeks to then introduce quantitative reasoning as a natural extension of qualitative reasoning. When reasoning quantitatively, students must learn to apply flexibly the full set of constraints available in circuit theory, and to reason "algebraically" in finding and applying multiple constraints.

1.3. An overview of the learning environment

Our QUEST (short for: Qualitative Understanding of Electrical System Troubleshooting) intelligent learning environment is a descendant of the SOPHIE [4] and STEAMER [23] intelligent tutoring systems: It makes use of interactive simulations, qualitative explanations, and a troubleshooting expert. However, unlike SOPHIE and STEAMER, QUEST is based upon a progression of qualitative models that correspond to the desired evolution of the learner's mental model. Furthermore, the interactive simulation of circuit behavior is driven by these qualitative models, and not by a quantitative model. Also, the system is capable of generating a runnable, qualitative, causal model for any circuit that the student or instructional designer might create (within the limits discussed in the next section). Thus students can, for example, use a circuit editor to create circuits and experiment with them. They can also ask the system to illustrate and explain the behavior of the circuit, or to demonstrate how to locate a fault within the circuit. In addition, there is a curriculum organized around the progression of models which serves to define classes of problems and facilitates the generation of explanations. Making use of this model progression, students can attempt to acquire an understanding of how circuits work in a more structured way, by solving problems designed to induce particular transformations in their understanding and by hearing explanations for how to solve those problems. They can also use the circuit editor to modify and experiment with these circuits presented to them by the system.

The instructional system thus provides students with a problem-solving environment within which circuits can be built, tested, and modified. The student can select circuit components from a list of devices that includes batteries, resistors, switches, fuses, light bulbs, wires, transistors, and capacitors. The student then places the device on the screen in the desired location and indicates its connections to other devices. At the same time, as the student is constructing a circuit diagram on the screen, the system is constructing a qualitative model of the circuit. The student can request that the model "run" in order to obtain a visual representation of circuit behavior and, if desired, a verbal explanation for the circuit's behavior (presented via computer generated speech and in written form on the display screen). Students can also use the circuit editor to experiment with circuits by changing the states of devices, inserting faults, and adding or deleting components.

The objective is to have the simulation describe the behavior of a circuit in both verbal and graphic terms. There are graphic icons for each device in the circuit which are represented on the display screen with the appropriate connections. When a fault is introduced into the circuit, both the device model and the graphic representation of the device change appropriately. For instance, shorts to ground alter the connectivity of the circuit, while opens alter the conductivity of the circuit. Similarly, when a device changes state, either as a result of an externally introduced change or as a result of the functioning of the circuit itself, the icon associated with that device can depict the new state. Furthermore, when the voltage redistribution processes operate, they can leave a visible trace of the path they are currently pursuing so that, for example, when they determine that there is a path with no resistance from a port of a device to ground, that path can be illustrated graphically on the display screen.

In addition to allowing the student to construct and modify circuits, the system makes available a progression of problem sets for the student to solve based upon the progression of mental models. Circuit problems given to students include (1) making predictions about circuit behavior, and (2) troubleshooting or isolating faults within circuits. Corresponding to each of these two types of problems are two tutoring facilities: (1) the qualitative, causal model of electrical circuits that underlies the simulation and can illustrate principles for reasoning about circuits; and (2) an "expert" troubleshooter that can demonstrate a strategy for isolating faults within circuits and that incorporates the same type of reasoning as that involved in predicting circuit behavior. The troubleshooting expert operates in interaction with the circuit model as it diagnoses faults.

When solving problems, students can call upon these programs to explain reasoning about circuit operation or troubleshooting logic. The qualitative simulation utilizes a model appropriate for the student at a given stage in learning and thus can articulate its reasoning at an appropriate level of explanation. When circuits with faults are introduced, the circuit model can explain to students the operation of such circuits in either their faulted or unfaulted condition. Explanations of troubleshooting logic produced by the troubleshooting expert are also coordinated in level of complexity with the explanations of circuit behavior offered by the circuit simulation.

1.4. An overview of the paper

In Section 1, we presented a theory of expertise and its evolution: learning can be regarded as a process of acquiring a set of coordinated mental models. We argued that in the initial stages of instruction, the models should be qualitative and causal. Constraints on model evolution, in terms of causal consistency and learnability, were discussed and a taxonomy of models useful for instruction was outlined. We then went on to provide an overview of our prototype intelligent learning environment based upon a progression of qualitative, causal mental models.

Section 2 describes the intelligence underlying our intelligent learning environment: the zero-order models of electrical circuit behavior and the troubleshooting expert. In presenting these models, we illustrate the instructional principles that governed their design. We conclude by describing the range of problem types that a tutoring system, or a human, possessing such expertise can solve. The reader who is not interested in the details of the qualitative models may choose to skip Section 2. Section 3 illustrates possible progressions, with respect to model elaboration, order, and perspective, in the context of presenting a theory of model evolution. Section 4 describes the simple architecture that enables the flexible pedagogical tools of the intelligent learning environment. The emphasis is on the range of instructional interactions and learning strategies that are supportable. Instructional trials of the system are then briefly discussed. Section 5 presents a summary of the paper.

2. The Models

2.1. The instructional need for zero-order models

The pioneering work of de Kleer [13] and others in [2] has shown how models can be developed that enable a computer to reason qualitatively about a physical domain. Further, these researchers have demonstrated that such models can be adequate to solve a large class of problems (e.g., de Kleer [14]). Our work on the design of qualitative models for instructional purposes has focused on creating models that (1) enable decompositions of sophisticated models into simpler models that can, nonetheless, accurately simulate the behavior of some class of circuits and can introduce basic circuit concepts and principles, and (2) enable the causality of circuit behaviors for the simpler models to be clear and at the same time compatible with that for more sophisticated models.

De Kleer's [14] EQUAL reasons in terms of qualitative derivatives obtained from qualitative versions of the constraint equations ("confluences") used in quantitative circuit analysis. These, together with several heuristics, enable it to analyze the effects of incremental change on circuit behavior. The difficulty with using such a model, at least at the initial stage of instruction, is that novices typically do not have well-developed concepts of voltage or resistance, let alone of changes in voltages or resistance [9, 10]. For example, as part of a trial of our instructional system, we interviewed seven high-school students who had not taken a physics course. They all initially exhibited serious misconceptions about circuit behaviors. For example, when asked to describe the behavior of the light in the circuit shown in Fig. 1 as the switches are opened and closed, only one of the seven students had a concept of a circuit.

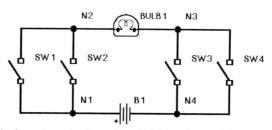

Fig. 1. A elementary circuit used in studying naive models of electricity.

The other students predicted that the bulb would light if only one of the switches were closed. A typical remark was the following, "If one of the switches on the left is closed, the light will light. It does not matter whether the switches on the right are open or closed." Further, they said, "If you close both switches on the left, the light will be twice as bright as if you close only one of them." In addition to this lack of a basic circuit concept, all seven of the students predicted that when you close the switch in Fig. 2, the light would still light—the statement that the switch has no resistance when closed did not matter. In fact, five of the students stated that they did not know what was meant by the term "resistance." They thus did not have the electrical concept of resistance and of how a nonresistive path could affect circuit behavior.

Novices such as these, who do not have accurate models of when a voltage is applied to a device in a circuit, could not possibly understand what is meant by a change in voltage across a device. Thus, we argue that students should

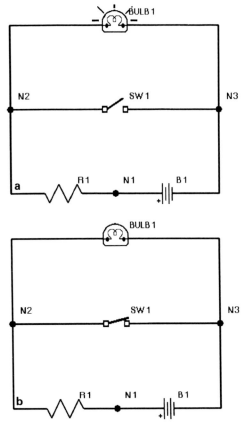

Fig. 2. An example of a circuit used to motivate model transformations.

initially be taught a progression of zero-order, qualitative models that reason about gross aspects of circuit behavior: the presence or absence of voltages in a circuit and their effect on the states of devices. This type of model can accurately simulate the behavior of a large class of circuits, and can be utilized to introduce fundamental ideas about circuit behavior.

The knowledge embedded in the zero-order models has been shown to be the type of knowledge that even college physics students lack [9], and is also crucial knowledge for successful troubleshooting. For example, consider an elementary form of troubleshooting such as trying to locate an open in the circuit shown in Fig. 3. Imagine that a test light is inserted into the middle of the circuit as shown in the figure. In order to make an inference about whether the open is in the part of the circuit in series with the test light or the part in parallel with it, one needs to know that if switch #1 were open, the light would *not* be on even if the circuit had no fault. Similarly, one needs to understand that if switch #2 were closed, the test light would *not* be on even if the circuit were unfaulted. Thus, even for performing the most elementary type of electrical troubleshooting, one needs a "zero-order understanding" of circuit behavior.

Once basic aspects of circuit behavior have been understood, students can then progress to analyzing more subtle aspects of circuit behavior. For example, they can learn to determine how increasing the resistance in a branch of a circuit increases and decreases voltages within the circuit. Such an analysis requires a more sophisticated form of qualitative reasoning that utilizes qualitative derivatives. The model is no longer simply reasoning about whether or not there is a voltage applied to a device; rather, it reasons about whether the voltage will increase or decrease. This type of analysis is necessary when analyzing, for instance, the occurrence of feedback within a circuit. Thus, the progression of qualitative models must evolve to incorporate "first-order reasoning," that is, reasoning about incremental changes. The first-order models utilize many of the features of the zero-order models and will be described in more detail later in the paper.

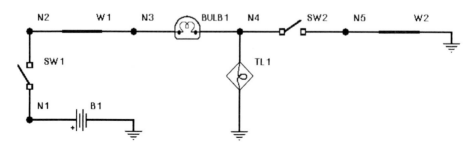

Fig. 3. Troubleshooting a simple series circuit with a test light.

2.2. The zero-order models

A progression of zero-order, behavioral models is implemented within our prototype intelligent learning environment. These models incorporate knowledge of (1) the topological structure of the circuit, (2) the behavior of the devices within the circuit (device models), and (3) basic electrical principles relating to the distribution of voltages within the circuit. These principles enable the model to reason about the effects of changes in the conductivity of circuit components, such as the effects of opening or closing a switch, on the voltages applied to other components of the circuit. The instructional system also includes a progression of general troubleshooting strategies for localizing faults within a circuit. These strategies utilize the behavioral models as part of their problem-solving process. Both the behavioral models and troubleshooting strategies can articulate their thinking, both visually and verbally, when simulating the behavior of a given circuit or when carrying out troubleshooting.

2.2.1. Circuit topology

The topology of the circuit is represented by the set of devices included in the circuit, together with the set of interconnections between designated ports of those devices. Thus, each instantiation of a device type within a circuit includes a table containing, for each of its ports, the electrical node to which it is connected.

Circuit parsing and orientation
The zero-order models utilize an algorithm that can parse any circuit, based upon its topology, into series and parallel subcircuits. This algorithm recursively recognizes and groups all series and parallel subcircuits by first bracketing all parallel subcircuits as units and then, working with what are currently the highest-level bracketed units, all series subcircuits. This process of alternately removing parallel and series subcircuits continues until no such subcircuits remain. In the case of bridge circuits, only parallel or series subcircuits within the circuit are grouped. In the case of series-parallel circuits, the final, top-level circuit is a series circuit. As the algorithm progresses, it also assigns conductivities to each of the subcircuits in the parse. The result is a hierarchical parsing of the circuit.

Establishing polarities of devices
Devices within the circuit are "oriented" by establishing polarities for each device and subcircuit. Polarities are assigned in relation to the voltage source, starting at the outermost grouping and moving inwards. Units contained within larger units are assigned the same polarities as those of the larger units which contain them.[3] The main purpose of the circuit orientation is to facilitate the

---

[3] The algorithm can identify indeterminacies in the assignment of polarities to a unit. For instance, if a unit has both feed paths to the positive side of a voltage source and return paths to
$\longrightarrow$

tracing of circuit paths and circuit loops. Since the circuits used in the initial stages of instruction are not very complex, and since humans have spatial skills that make circuit tracing generally quite effortless, circuit orientation is not explicitly taught until necessary.

2.2.2. *Device models*

The zero-order models contain models for devices typically found in circuits. The devices modeled are batteries, switches, resistors, bulbs, diodes, fuses, capacitors, transistors, test lights, and wires. Device models include rules for determining a device's *state*, based upon the circuit environment of the device. For example, if there is a voltage drop across the two ports of a light bulb, the light bulb will be in the "on" state; otherwise it is in the "off" state. The conditions for the rules that determine device states are written in such a way that only one of them can be true at a given point in time and they are evaluated in parallel, so that, on a given evaluation, only one of the rules will be executed. When a device's state changes, the device model activates additional rules which re-evaluate a set of *state variables* associated with the device. These variables include (1) the conductivity of the device (is it purely conductive,[4] conductive but resistive, or nonconductive), and (2) whether or not the device is a source of voltage. For example, when a capacitor is in the charged state, it is nonconductive and a source of voltage. Finally, the device models include *fault states*, which include rules for altering the device variables to make them consistent with a particular fault, and which override the normal states for the device. For example, when a light bulb is faulted "open," it becomes nonconductive and its state will be "off." Some illustrations of device models[5] follow:

Battery

States: Charged or Discharged.

If the battery is discharged and if it has a voltage applied to it, then it becomes charged; otherwise it remains discharged.

If the battery is charged and if there is a path with no resistive elements across the battery, then it becomes discharged; otherwise it remains charged.

$\longrightarrow$

the negative side of a voltage source from *each* of its ports, then its orientation may not be determined. If all of these paths lead to the same voltage source, it is a bridge element in the circuit. If the paths lead to different voltage sources having different polarities, the orientation of the unit is also indeterminate (see [36]).

[4] The term "purely conductive" is introduced to represent the conductivity of devices such as wires, whose resistance is very much lower than that of other circuit components.

[5] The devices are modeled as ideal components. Thus, for example, the battery is modeled as purely conductive because an ideal battery as a pure voltage source has no resistance, even though, real world batteries are resistive.

Internal Conductivity: Purely-Conductive.

Voltage Source:
   If the battery is charged, then it is a source of voltage; otherwise it is not.

Fault Example: Permanently Discharged.
   If the fault is permanently discharged, then set its status as a voltage source to permanently nil.

For relatively complex devices such as capacitors, it is unrealistic to expect students at the outset to acquire the most sophisticated device models. Students are therefore introduced to a progression of increasingly sophisticated and adequate models for such devices.[6] The initial capacitor model is illustrated below. It should be noted that when a device state change occurs during a given causal propagation cycle, it takes some indeterminate amount of time. Thus when the capacitor goes from the charged state to the discharged state, it can serve as a voltage source during that propagation cycle as illustrated further in Section 2.2.4.

Capacitor

State: Charged or Discharged.
   If it has a voltage applied to it, then its state is charged.
   If it does not have a voltage applied to it and:
   – if its state is discharged, then it remains discharged.
   – if its state is charged and if it has a conductive path across it, then its state becomes discharged; otherwise it remains charged.

---

[6] The initial capacitor model only incorporates two discrete states: charged and discharged. One limitation of such a zero-order capacitor model is that it does not explicitly introduce the nonsteady states of charging and discharging. Furthermore, a capacitor is not just "charged," rather it is "charged to a given voltage." So, for example, if it is being charged by a small battery, it becomes charged to a low voltage, whereas, if it is being charged by a higher voltage battery, it becomes charged to a high voltage. The consequence is that when a capacitor is charged to a given voltage, it is conductive-resistive to voltage sources higher than that voltage and is nonconductive to lower voltage sources. Thus the internal conductivity and resistance of the capacitor, which can affect the behavior of other devices in the circuit, can only be determined by knowing the level to which the capacitor is charged. For circuits with only one voltage source and for certain circuits with multiple voltage sources, circuit behavior can be accurately simulated without making this distinction. However, more complex circuits require the distinction to be made and thus learning about capacitors can motivate the need to understand more complex aspects of circuit behavior. They also can be used to introduce the limits of qualitative models and motivate the need for quantitative models. For example, consider a case where there are two low-level batteries in series. The model now needs a rule saying that two voltage sources in series add together, but, what is LOW + LOW? Even further, what is LOW + HIGH? This illustrates a fundamental limitation of models that utilize category scales.

Internal Conductivity:
    If it is charged, then it is nonconductive in the polarity with which it is charged, but it is purely conductive in the opposite polarity.
    If it is discharged, then it is purely conductive.

Voltage Source:
    If it is charged, then it is a source of voltage.
    If it is discharged, then it is not a source of voltage.

Fault Example: Internally Shorted.
    If the capacitor is internally shorted, then set its internal conductivity to purely conductive and its status as a source of voltage to nil.

When a particular device, such as a capacitor, is employed within a particular circuit, a data table is created for the specific instantiation of that device in that circuit. This table is used to record (1) the present state of the device, (2) whether it is presently a voltage source, (3) its internal conductivity (what possible internal conductive paths exist among its ports and whether they are presently purely conductive, resistive, or nonconductive), (4) the device polarity, and (5) its fault status. When the student is performing a mental simulation of a particular circuit, the student must also keep track of this information. The information must be recorded, either above the device in the circuit diagram, in a device data table (as illustrated in Fig. 5), or in memory. Most of the circuits we use to introduce basic circuit concepts and laws are simple enough that the student can remember this information—especially since the student is typically focusing on the behavior of one device, such as a light bulb.

A mental model for a device, of the form illustrated for batteries and capacitors, enables the student to determine the state of the device for any circuit environment in which it is placed.[7] Information related to the state of the device, such as its internal conductivity and whether or not it is a source of voltage, will in turn affect the behavior of other devices in the circuit. Such a device model will thus form the basis for understanding the causality of circuit behavior in terms of showing how a change in state of one device can produce a change in state of another device within the circuit. It does not, however, provide the student with a "complete" understanding of how a battery or capacitor works. For example, the capacitor model cannot generate an explanation for why a capacitor becomes nonconductive when it is charged. One ultimately needs to introduce, in addition to behavioral models, physical models for devices.

---

[7] It should be noted that the behavior of the device will be accurate within the limits of the adequacy of the device model. Thus for complex circuits, a more sophisticated capacitor model may be required.

2.2.3. *Circuit principles employed*

Device models re-evaluate their states on the basis of the voltages that are currently being applied to them in the simulation. Whenever a change occurs in a device's state, a change may also occur in the device's conductivity or its status as a voltage source. These changes in turn effect the distribution of voltages within the circuit and, consequently, the voltages that are being applied to other circuit devices. The qualitative simulation employs general circuit principles for propagating the effects of these changes in a device's state on the voltages applied to other devices. We have developed two alternative forms for carrying out this propagation: (1) a *device-centered* causal propagation in which devices effectively ask themselves, "What effect did device X's change in state have on me?" and (2) a *process-centered* causal propagation where any change in device state triggers an explicit voltage redistribution process. Forbus [21] has argued for the utility of process-centered models in making the causality of physical systems more explicit. We argue that both propagation mechanisms have their utility in instruction, in problem solving, and in unpacking the causality of circuit behavior. For instance, the device-centered mechanism enables one to focus on the behavior of a single device, and by so doing to introduce basic concepts such as that of a circuit. In addition, when solving circuit problems such as in troubleshooting, this approach enables one to focus on the behavior of a single device such as a test light and to envision what possible faults would do its behavior. On the other hand, the process-centered mechanism enables one to see more explicitly the redistribution of voltages that can occur when a device changes state, and is more efficient when envisioning the behavior of large circuits.

2.2.4. *The device-centered propagation*

In this control logic, whenever any device's internal conductivity or status as a voltage source changes, all of the other devices in the circuit re-evaluate their states. This allows any changes in conductivity or presence of voltage sources within the circuit to propagate their effects to the states of other devices.[8] If in the course of this re-evaluation some additional devices change state, then the re-evaluation process is repeated. This series of propagation cycles continues until the behavior of the circuit stabilizes and no further changes in device states have occurred. Whenever any further changes in device internal conductivity or status as a voltage source occur, due either to the passage of time or to external intervention, the propagation of state changes commences once again.

---

[8] The circuit information used for this re-evaluation is the set of device data tables existing at the initiation of the re-evaluation (not those that are being created in the current re-evaluation cycle). This is to avoid unwanted sequential dependencies in determining device states.

Circuit principles

In order for a device model to re-evaluate its state, it must establish whether or not it currently has a voltage applied to it. To do this, the device models call upon rules to determine, based upon the circuit topology and the states of devices, whether or not the device has a voltage applied to it. The most sophisticated Zero-Order Voltage Rule is based on the concept that, for a device to have a voltage applied to it, it must occur in a circuit (loop) containing a voltage source and must not have any nonresistive paths in parallel with it within that circuit. More formally, the Zero-Order Voltage Rule can be stated as:

> If there is at least one conductive path to the negative side of a voltage source from one port of the device (a return path), and if there is a conductive path from another port of the device to the positive side of that voltage source (a feed path), with no nonresistive path branching from any point on that "feed" path to any point on any "return" path, then, the device has a voltage applied to that pair of ports.[9]

Changes in a circuit, such as closing a switch, can alter in a dramatic way, the conductivity of the circuit and thereby produce changes in whether or not a device has a voltage applied to it. To illustrate, when the switch is open in the circuit shown in Fig. 2(a), the device model for the light bulb calls upon procedures for evaluating voltages in order to determine whether the light's state is on or off. The procedure finds a good feed path and a good return path and thus the light bulb will be on. When the switch is closed, as shown in Fig. 2(b), the procedure finds a short from the feed to the return path and thus the light bulb will be off.

Topological search

The rules that embody circuit principles, such as the Zero-Order Voltage Rule utilize topological search processes that are needed, for example, to determine whether a device has a conductive path to a source of voltage. The search processes utilize the information maintained by the device data tables concerning the devices' circuit connections, polarity, internal conductivity, and whether or not they serve as voltage sources. The topological search processes can locate conductive paths within the circuit. For example, they can find all conductive paths from one port of a device to another port of the same device, or to a port of another device. They can also check to see if the paths are resistive or nonresistive. The students execute analogous search processes

---

[9] By "voltage applied to a device," we mean the qualitative version of the open circuit (or Thevenin) voltage, that is, the voltage the device sees as it looks into the circuit. In the case of the Zero-Order Voltage Rule, this is simply the presence or absence of voltage.

when tracing from one device to another, using the circuit diagram, in order to locate, for instance, a feed path for a device.

A sample zero-order circuit simulation
As an illustration of how this zero-order model reasons, consider a simulation of the behavior of the circuit illustrated in Fig. 4:

> Initially suppose that both switches are open, the light bulb is off, and the capacitor is discharged. Then, suppose that someone closes switch #1. This change in the internal conductivity of a device causes the other devices in the circuit to re-evaluate their states. The capacitor remains discharged because switch #2 being open prevents it from having a good return path. The light bulb has good feed and return paths, so its state becomes on. Since, in the course of this re-evaluation no device changed its conductivity, the re-evaluation process terminates. Note that even though the light bulb changed state, its internal conductivity is always the same, so its change of state can have no effect on circuit behavior and thus does not trigger the re-evaluation process.
>
> Now, imagine that someone closes switch #2. This change in state produces a change in the conductivity of the switch and triggers the re-evaluation process. The light bulb attempts to re-evaluate its state and finds that its feed path is shorted out by the capacitor (which is purely conductive because it is in the discharged state) and switch #2 (which is also purely conductive because its state is closed), so its state becomes off. The capacitor attempts to re-evaluate its state and finds that it has a good feed and return path, so its state becomes charged. This change in state causes it to

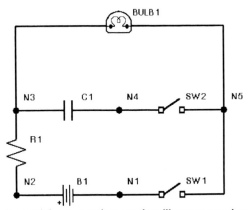

Fig. 4. A circuit containing a capacitor, used to illustrate causal propagations.

re-evaluate its internal conductivity, and to re-evaluate whether it is a source of voltage. As a result of the capacitor becoming charged, it becomes nonconductive, and a source of voltage. This change in the internal conductivity of the capacitor causes the re-evaluation process to trigger again. The light bulb re-evaluates its state and finds that it has a good feed and return path (it is no longer shorted out by the capacitor because the capacitor is now charged and therefore nonconductive) and its state becomes on. This change in the light bulb's state has no effect on the light bulb's internal conductivity so the re-evaluation process terminates.

Suppose that someone then opens switch #1. This changes the switches internal conductivity and therefore causes all other devices to re-evaluate their states. The light bulb no longer has a good return path with respect to the battery. However, it has a good feed and return path to another source of voltage within the circuit, the capacitor (which is charged and therefore a source of voltage). The state of the light bulb will thus be on. The capacitor no longer has a good return path to a source of voltage and it has a conductive path across it, so its state becomes discharged and it becomes purely conductive and is not a source of voltage. This change in the capacitors internal conductivity causes the light bulb to re-evaluate its state. Since the capacitor is no longer a source of voltage, and since switch #1 is open thereby preventing a good return path to the battery, the light bulb concludes that its state is off. This change in state has no effect on the light bulb's internal conductivity so the re-evaluation process terminates.

Notice that this relatively unsophisticated qualitative simulation has been able to simulate and explain some important aspects of this circuit's behavior. It demonstrates how, when switch #2 is closed, it initially shorts out the bulb, and then, when the capacitor charges, it no longer shorts out the bulb. Further, it explains how, when switch #1 is open, the capacitor causes the light bulb to light initially, and then, when the capacitor becomes discharged, the light bulb goes out. The behavior is summarized in Figs. 5 and 6.

The evolution of the control structure
By control structure we mean the determination of what goal to pursue next when reasoning about the behavior of a circuit (what Anderson et al. [1] term the "problem-solving structure"). An example of control knowledge within the qualitative model is, "when one device changes its conductivity, all other devices in the circuit must re-evaluate their states." The system makes such control knowledge clear to the student by simply reasoning out loud. For instance, it might state, "I am trying to determine whether this device has a voltage applied to it (i.e., it states a goal). In order to do that, I must search

Device	Variables	Initial Conditions	TIME →							
Switch 1	State	Open	Closed	Closed	Closed	Closed	Closed	Open	Open	Open
	Conductivity	N-C	P-C*	P-C	P-C	P-C	P-C	N-C*	N-C	N-C
	Voltage Source	No	No	No	No	No	No	No	No	No
Switch 2	State	Open	Open	Open	Closed	Closed	Closed	Closed	Closed	Closed
	Conductivity	N-C	N-C	N-C	P-C*	P-C	P-C	P-C	P-C	P-C
	Voltage Source	No	No	No	No	No	No	No	No	No
Capacitor	State	Discharged	Discharged	Discharged	Discharged	Charged	Charged	Charged	Discharged	Discharged
	Conductivity	P-C	P-C	P-C	P-C	N-C*	N-C	N-C	P-C*	P-C
	Voltage Source	No	No	No	No	Yes*	Yes	Yes	No*	No
Light Bulb	State	Off	Off	On	On	Off	On	On	On	Off
	Conductivity	C-R	C-R	C-R	C-R	C-R	C-R	C-R	C-R	C-R
	Voltage Source	No	No	No	No	No	No	No	No	No
Resistor	State	Cold	Cold	Hot	Hot	Hot	Hot	Hot	Cold	Cold
	Conductivity	C-R	C-R	C-R	C-R	C-R	C-R	C-R	C-R	C-R
	Voltage Source	No	No	No	No	No	No	No	No	No
Battery	State	Charged	Charged	Charged	Charged	Charged	Charged	Charged	Charged	Charged
	Conductivity	P-C	P-C	P-C	P-C	P-C	P-C	P-C	P-C	P-C
	Voltage Source	Yes	Yes	Yes	Yes	Yes	Yes	Yes	Yes	Yes

LEGEND:
Conductivity = Non-Conductive (N-C), Purely-Conductive (P-C), or Conductive-Resitive (C-R)

□ = Device Changed State

* = Device's internal conductivity or status as a voltage source changed which triggers a reevaluation cycle

▊ = Circuit behavior stabilizes, i.e., end of a sequence of reevaluation cycles

Fig. 5. A history of device data tables that represents the behavior of the circuit shown in Fig. 4.

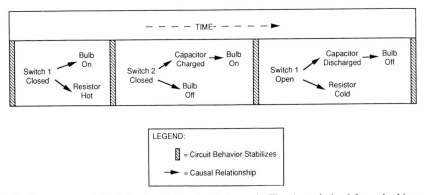

LEGEND:

▊ = Circuit Behavior Stabilizes

➤ = Causal Relationship

Fig. 6. A summary of the behavior of the circuit shown in Fig. 4, as derived from the history of device data tables shown in Fig. 5.

for a conductive path from one port of the device to a voltage source. Then, I must . . . (i.e., it states the means for achieving its goal)." Thus the system articulates its goals and subgoals, as well as its means for achieving those goals. By so doing, the control structure of the causal propagation becomes apparent to the student.

When the student is attempting to predict the behavior of a single device within a circuit such as a test light, it is sometimes necessary to know the states of other devices within the circuit: If there are devices such as capacitors and transistors whose internal conductivity is state-dependent, then their state must be determined in order to determine the state of the light bulb. Thus, even for this simple type of problem, a mental simulation of the entire circuit can be necessary.

The complexity of the control structure required for simulating circuit behavior varies with the type of circuit. For circuits that contain only devices like resistors and bulbs whose internal conductivity does not change when their states change, a serial re-evaluation of device states is all that is necessary. However, for circuits containing multiple devices, such as capacitors and transistors, whose internal conductivity changes when their state changes, parallel re-evaluation of device states is crucial for accurately simulating the behavior of the circuit. One approach is for students to simulate parallelism the way the computer model does by using device data tables as shown in Fig. 5. Students learn that the device whose change precipitated the re-evaluation does not get re-evaluated, so that its data remain the same while other devices undergo re-evaluation. The remaining devices use the present data of other devices in the circuit, not the re-evaluated data, when re-evaluating their own state. By circling the devices that change state on each propagation cycle (i.e., each column of the table), the sequence of state changes for the circuit can become clear as illustrated in Figs. 5 and 6.

The device-centered propagation becomes lengthy for large circuits. A second approach that is more efficient, and more direct in terms of the causality of circuit behavior, is the process-centered approach described below.

2.2.5. *The process-centered propagation*

In this approach, the circuit principles are embedded in a process called voltage redistribution. This uses rules based upon Kirchhoff's Voltage Law to immediately propagate "forward" the effects of a change in conductivity of a device on voltages applied to other devices in the circuit. Then, only those other devices whose applied voltages have changed will undergo re-evaluation. Furthermore, since it will already have been established whether or not there is a voltage being applied to each device, redundant searches for paths to a voltage source are avoided. This approach of immediately propagating the effects of changes in a device's conductivity on the distribution of voltages is more closely related to the causality of our reductionistic, physical model, which focuses on the voltage redistribution process.

Rules for circuit loops
The propagation logic for redistributing voltages within a circuit begins by applying rules for assigning voltages within circuit loops containing a voltage

source. These loops are those in the top-level of the circuit parse, and are typically made up of a combination of devices and bracketed subcircuits (together referred to as components of the loop). If there are no nonconductive components in the loop (i.e., the loop is conductive), voltage drops are assigned to all resistive components. While no voltage drops occur across purely conductive components,[10] they nonetheless have voltages applied to them. These rules apply to conductive circuit loops. If, on the other hand, the circuit loop contains one or more nonconductive components, a voltage drop is assigned only across the nonconductive segment of the circuit.

Rules for subcircuits

Next, if any components of the loop to which voltages have been assigned consist of *subcircuits*, then voltages remain to be redistributed within those subcircuits. Rules for doing this depend upon the conductivity of the subcircuit. For example, if the subcircuit contains a purely conductive path, then no components of the subcircuit will have voltage drops and only components of the purely conductive path within the subcircuit will have voltages applied to them. On the other hand, if the subcircuit is resistive, then voltage drops are assigned to all resistive components within its conductive paths. For any nonconductive paths, the voltage drop will occur across the nonconductive segment of the path. Similar rules are applied if the subcircuit is nonconductive.

Control structure

Whenever a device changes its conductivity, one first updates the conductivities of any subcircuits containing that device. Then the rules for assigning voltages within circuit loops are applied for all loops containing components whose conductivity (or status as a voltage source) has changed. Next, voltages are redistributed within subcircuits of those loops for which the voltage has changed. If the result of the above voltage redistribution process causes a change in voltage across a component of some intersecting circuit loop, then a further voltage redistribution is carried out within that loop, and so on. Finally, once the voltages have been redistributed, those devices for which there have been changes in applied voltages are prompted to re-evaluate their states. If any of these change their conductivity or status as a voltage source, another propagation cycle begins. Propagations cease when the circuit behavior stabilizes.

---

[10] Since devices having very low resistance are regarded as purely conductive within the zero-order model, they will have no voltage drop across them even when they are in a circuit loop in which they have a voltage applied to them. For purely conductive devices, it is therefore necessary to keep track of applied voltages. For devices that are resistive or nonconductive, there will always be an applied voltage whenever there is a voltage drop across them.

An example of circuit simulation using voltage redistribution
As an illustration of how this zero-order model reasons, we will apply it to the
same circuit analyzed earlier (see Fig. 4).

We will begin with the case where switch #2 is open and switch #1
is closed. First, voltages are distributed within the series circuit loop
made up of the battery, the resistor, the parallel subcircuit (containing the light bulb, connected across the capacitor and switch #2),
and switch #1. Since all of these three circuit components are
conductive, voltage drops are assigned across the two resistive
components (the resistor and the subcircuit). Switch #1 has no
voltage drop across it, since it is regarded as purely conductive,
although it does have a voltage applied to it. Second, voltages are
assigned within the parallel subcircuit. Since the subcircuit has a
voltage across it, resistive components within its conductive path
(here, the light bulb) also have voltages across them. However,
within the nonconductive path, the voltage drop appears only
across the nonconductive segment (here switch #2) and no voltage
is applied to the capacitor. Since the light bulb has a voltage applied
to it, it enters the "on" state.

Next, we will suppose that switch #2 is closed. Since there has
been a change in its conductivity, the conductivity of the subcircuit
containing it has to be revised. Since the capacitor (which is initially
discharged) and switch #2 are both purely conductive, the subcircuit contains a purely conductive path and is therefore also
purely conductive. Within the circuit loop containing the battery,
the subcircuit now has no voltage drop across it (since it is purely
conductive), although it has a voltage applied to it. This implies
that, within the subcircuit, any circuit paths connected across the
purely conductive path cannot have voltages applied to them, and
only components within the purely conductive path can have voltages applied to them. Changes in voltages thus occur for two
devices: the light bulb and the capacitor. These devices therefore
are prompted to re-evaluate their states. The light bulb no longer
has a voltage applied to it and goes from the "on" to the "off" state
(but does not change in conductivity), while the capacitor now has
a voltage applied to it and goes from the discharged to the charged
state. This causes it to change in conductivity from purely conductive to nonconductive (it also becomes a source of voltage).

These changes in state of the capacitor cause another redistribution of voltages within the circuit. First, since the subcircuit containing the capacitor changes from being purely conductive to resistive,
and since it remains in a conductive loop with the battery, it now

has a voltage across it. Consequently, within the subcircuit there are now voltage drops across the capacitor and light bulb, neither of which is purely conductive. Second, since the capacitor is now a voltage source, and since it is in a conductive loop with the light bulb and switch #2, it will also apply a voltage to the light bulb. Since the polarity of this voltage drop is the same as that previously assigned, there is no ambiguity and the voltage can be assigned to the light bulb. Finally, since the light bulb now has a change in its voltage, it re-evaluates its state, this time going from off to on. As this state change does not alter its conductivity, no further changes in the distribution of voltages occur and the circuit behavior stabilizes.

2.3. Model limitations

Two limitations of these qualitative models emerge when multiple events occur on the same propagation cycle. For example, imagine that on a given cycle a transistor becomes saturated and a capacitor becomes charged. The first difficulty relates to determining the order of the events and the second relates to determining the cause of subsequent events.

Time. A major limitation of qualitative models is that the sequencing of events happens in ordinal, not interval, time. That is, the state changes happen in a given order, but the length of time such events take is indeterminate. For instance, if closing a switch causes a transistor to now have a voltage drop across its base-emitter path, how long does it take for the transistor to become saturated? Is it an instant or a relatively long time? The simulation has no way of knowing. Further, imagine that closing that same switch causes a voltage drop not only across a transistor, but also across a capacitor. According to the model, the transistor becomes saturated and the capacitor becomes charged. Both events are caused by closing the switch and happen on the same propagation cycle. However, the two events do not necessarily take the same amount of time. Thus, it could be the case that the transistor becomes saturated before the capacitor becomes charged, or vice versa, or both new states could be reached at the same time. To further complicate matters, for certain circuits, the subsequent behavior will vary depending upon which of these possibilities occurs. Thus, accurately simulating their behavior will depend crucially on distinguishing between these possibilities. In such cases, all zero-order, qualitative models can do is to articulate the range of possible behaviors for the circuit. If the capacitor becomes charged at a certain point with respect to the behavior of the transistor, the circuit will exhibit one behavior, whereas, if it becomes charged at another point, the circuit will exhibit a different behavior. The student, or system, must then use knowledge about the purpose of the circuit, knowledge about the relative times for events to occur, or quantitative models to determine what is the likely behavior for such a circuit.

Cause. This multiplicity of events occurring within a given propagation cycle raises yet another model limitation. Imagine, for the sake of argument, that the transistor and capacitor in the above example reach their new states at the same time, or, alternatively, that in another circuit, someone closes two switches simultaneously. Further, imagine that on the next propagation cycle for either circuit, another device, such as a light bulb, changes state. In each case, was it the change in state of device #1, or device #2, or both that caused the light bulb to change state? The device-centered propagation could unpack the causality by keeping histories of feed and return paths for each device. The model could then investigate these histories to determine whether the state change for device #1 and/or device #2 completed or destroyed a feed and/or return path for the light bulb. Alternatively, one could hypothesize that only device #1 or device #2 changed state and then envision whether the test light would have changed state under either of these conditions.

These limitations and complexities of zero-order, qualitative models in producing the correct sequence of state changes and unpacking circuit causality are serious from a simulation perspective. Yet, from an instructional perspective they are not. It is the limits of particular models that help to define pedagogically appropriate classes of problems. For instance, when designing sequences of circuit problems to tutor the concepts of resistance, voltage, and the voltage redistribution process, it is not necessary to introduce circuits so complex as to broach these complexities. In fact, to do so would be poor instructional design. This again argues for the utility of qualitative models, not only for introducing fundamental circuit concepts and principles, but also for being able to define the problem context in which they should be introduced.

2.4. Model strengths

We sought models that would be powerful enough to enable the system and the students to envision and explain circuit behavior. We also sought models that would be robust in permitting faults to be introduced or circuits to be modified without requiring a new model for each perturbation in the circuit. Finally, unlike de Kleer [14], we wanted to avoid making assumptions about the integrity of the circuit and, therefore, to avoid running into contradictions during the envisioning process.

No-function-in-structure. By utilizing context-free models for devices along with circuit principles for determining the distribution of voltages, we have been able to construct qualitative circuit models that simulate the behavior of a large class of circuits in both faulted and unfaulted states. The device models are prototypical and behave appropriately (within the limits discussed) in whatever circuit they are placed. The only circuit-specific information that is required is the set of device interconnections, that is, information about the structure of the particular circuit. Similarly, the circuit principles embody general laws of circuit behavior that work (again within the limits discussed) for all circuits. Thus our models are in keeping with de Kleer and Brown's [15] no-function-in-structure principle.

Creating knowledge structures that follow this principle is important in enabling the system's qualitative model to simulate and generate explanations for the behavior of any circuit that the students choose to construct. It is also an important property for the students' mental models in that it ensures that their knowledge will then be in a form that enables them to understand and predict the behavior of any circuit.

In addition to obeying the no-function-in-structure principle, the model's control structure, circuit principles, and the format for device models are general and compatible with higher-order models. Thus, when students are introduced to a new type of circuit (e.g., logic circuits) incorporating new types of devices (e.g., logic gates), they should be able to generalize their knowledge to this new situation. Moreover, they should be able to transfer their knowledge of model form and process to the acquisition of new models of circuit behavior (such as first-order models that involve incremental qualitative reasoning). Generality thus enhances the learnability of new models that are extensions of the earlier models.

Finally, one of the most impressive features of the type of qualitative, causal models described in this paper is its utility in helping to solve a wide range of circuit problems. For example, the student can be asked to predict the state of a single device, to describe the behavior of the entire circuit, or to determine what faults are possible given the behavior of the circuit. Further, students can be asked to locate a faulty component within a circuit, or to design a circuit. The ability to perform this type of model-based simulation of circuit behavior is instrumental in solving all of these types of problems.

2.5. The troubleshooting expert

The problem of troubleshooting a circuit requires students to reason "on their feet" about circuit behavior, and is potentially a very powerful instructional task. Conventionally, however, troubleshooting is preceded by instruction on circuit theory, rather than used as a vehicle for teaching models of circuit behavior. By decomposing troubleshooting strategies along lines that are parallel to those used in the construction of zero-order qualitative models, troubleshooting problems can be incorporated within the general instructional sequence.

The progression of troubleshooting strategies is based upon a qualitative approach taken by an expert whom we have studied. This expert not only utilizes this approach in actual diagnostic work, but also teaches the technique to students in a technical high school. The methods he uses are based upon the fundamental idea of a circuit, and employ circuit principles that are similar to those of the zero-order model (which was motivated in part by the approach of this expert): For a device to "operate" (e.g., for a test light to light or a capacitor to charge), it must have voltage applied to it. In order for there to be voltage applied to a device, there must be a source of voltage, and conductive paths leading from each port of the device to, respectively, the positive and negative sides of the voltage source. In a series circuit, one source of faults is the occurrence of opens within either of these paths. Another source of faults is the presence of shorts to ground, which introduce nonresistive parallel paths into the circuit. If these shorts occur between the device and the ungrounded (usually positive) side of the voltage source, they will prevent voltages from being applied to the device. These two types of faults, opens and shorts to ground, are the ones that the troubleshooting expert is designed to diagnose.

The strategy used by the expert is a "space splitting" strategy. Its goal is to divide the circuit into two parts and then to infer which portion of the circuit contains the fault. Once the fault has been isolated to one or the other segment, then the troubleshooting logic is recursively applied to the faulty segment. The process continues until the fault has been localized.

This top level strategy is accomplished using the following approach: First, for purposes of measurement and inference, the circuit is logically divided into two parts by inserting a test light near the center of the circuit (i.e., between the test point and the grounded (negative) side of the voltage source). As can be seen in Fig. 3, this places the test light in series with one segment of the circuit (that between the positive side of the voltage source and the test point) and in parallel with the other segment (that between the test point and the grounded side of the voltage source). Next, the circuit simulation is run to determine the correct state of the test light if the circuit had no fault. That state is then compared with the actual test light behavior, and inferences are made about possible faults that are consistent with the findings.[11] Additional troubleshooting operations are then carried out to isolate the fault possibilities to either the portion of the circuit in series with the test light, or the one in parallel with it.[12] When the fault possibilities have been isolated to within a particular segment of the circuit, the expert moves the test light to a new test

---

[11] These inferences depend upon whether or not the test light is supposed to be on given an unfaulted circuit, and upon the actual behavior of the light in the presence of the fault. For instance, if the test light is supposed to be on but is not on, the fault could be either an open or a short to ground in the part of the circuit in series with the test light, or it could be a short to ground in the part of the circuit in parallel with the test light (at a point before any resistance is encountered).

[12] In the example shown in Fig. 3, the expert detaches switch SW2 from N4, and observes the effect. If the test light comes on, the fault has been isolated to the portion of the circuit in parallel with the test light. More particularly, it was providing a nonresistive path from the feed path of the test light to the ground, and thus shorting out the test light. If the test light remains off, the problem must be an open or a short to ground in the portion of the circuit in series with the test light.

point within the faulty segment of the circuit and reapplies the troubleshooting logic. In selecting the next test point, the troubleshooting expert may again apply the strategy of dividing the circuit in half, or it may instead employ a serial strategy of simply moving the test light, one component at a time, away from the earlier test point. This process is repeated until the fault is located.

The troubleshooting logic as described here is restricted to series circuits. However, additional principles allow it to be extended to parallel circuits and to series-parallel circuits. In instruction, the troubleshooting strategy presented to students increases progressively in complexity, in coordination with the progression of behavioral circuit models that the students acquire (see [47]).

2.5.1. *Facilitating troubleshooting*

The faults that can be introduced into a circuit in the current version of the instructional system are shorts to ground and opens. Each device model has rules for determining how each fault will alter its data. For instance, shorts to ground change the circuit connections for the device whereas opens may change the conductivity of the device. Both types of fault can change the state of the device. When a particular fault is removed from the circuit, the device data are returned to their unfaulted values and the circuit simulation proceeds on that basis. The particular faults that are introduced at any stage in instruction are chosen to be consistent with the capabilities of the student's (and the system's) present model of circuit behavior. Thus, for instance, shorts to ground are not introduced until students have learned about nonresistive parallel paths.

To facilitate troubleshooting, a test light can be introduced by the student into a circuit. In addition, any port of a device can be disconnected (for example, one can choose to disconnect the portion of a circuit in parallel with a test light). These troubleshooting operations alter the circuit connections, and the model simulates the behavior of the circuit accordingly. The availability of these facilities enables students to troubleshoot for themselves. If at any time they want assistance, they can call upon the system "expert" to demonstrate its techniques on the circuit they are working on and explain its logic. In fact, if they choose they can themselves plant a fault into a circuit and have the expert demonstrate how it would proceed to isolate it.

2.6. Problem-solving capabilities

One of the most impressive features of an intelligent learning environment based upon causal models and problem-solving experts is the range of problem types for which the system's (and the student's) expertise is applicable. The following describes the types of problems supportable by an environment based upon the causal models and troubleshooting expert described in the previous sections.

Predicting the effects of a change in state: *Envisioning circuit behavior*
The student is presented with a circuit and is asked to predict the behavior of a
device or devices in the circuit. Similarly, for certain model transformations,
the student or computer can insert test lights into various points in the circuit
and the student is asked to predict the behavior of the test light. In addition,
the student or the computer may change the state of some device (e.g. open or
close a switch), or fault a device, and the student is again asked to predict the
behavior of the light. The system gives the student feedback concerning
whether his or her prediction was correct or incorrect. Also, the student is
given the option of having the system give its explanation as to what the state
of the device or devices is and why.

Determining the possible origins of a given behavior: *Enumerating all
possible faults consistent with circuit behavior*
The student is presented with a circuit containing a fault unknown to the
student and a test light inserted into the circuit between a particular point and
ground (as in Fig. 3). The student is then asked to enumerate all possible faults
that are consistent with the behavior of the test light. When the student has
finished selecting all faults that he or she believes would produce the given test
light behavior, the student is given feedback concerning the correctness of her
or his selections as well as any omissions he or she has made. At any point in
the problem-solving process, the student can request to have an unfaulted
circuit to work with, complete with the test light, and can experiment with
introducing faults into the circuit and observing the behavior of the test light.
As in the prediction problems, the student can also request that the system give
an explanation of why the test light is in that state. In addition, the student can
request to hear the system solve the problem, which it can do by hypothesizing
all possible faults and running the qualitative simulation to see what test light
behavior results. In doing so, it considers five possible fault types and
locations, (1) an open in the part of the circuit in series with the test light, (2) a
short to ground in the part of the circuit in series with the test light, (3) an
open in the part of the circuit in parallel with the test light, (4) a short to
ground in the part of the circuit in parallel with the test light before a point
where resistance is encountered, and (5) a short to ground in the part of the
circuit in parallel with the test light after a point where resistance is encountered. If the test light behavior for any of these fault possibilities is
consistent with the given behavior of the test light, then that fault is included in
the set of possible faults that are consistent with the test light behavior.

Isolating the cause of an unexpected behavior: *Troubleshooting problems*
The system selects a fault for a given circuit and the student is asked to
determine the location and type of fault. The student can insert a test light
between any point in the circuit and ground. The student can also disconnect
devices from one another. After each such operation that the student per-

forms, he or she is asked two questions [19]: (1) given the current behavior of the test light, which portion of the circuit, that in parallel or that in series with the test light (or both), could contain (i) an open or (ii) a short to ground, and (2) can you determine the specific location of the fault yet, and if so where is it? When the student has located the fault, the computer gives the student feedback as to whether the choice is right or wrong. At any point in the troubleshooting process, the student can request to hear how the computer would troubleshoot the circuit.

Restructuring in order to achieve a particular behavior: Circuit design and modification problems

The student is asked to create, using the circuit construction kit, a circuit that achieves a particular purpose. For example, when learning about nonresistive parallel paths, the student could be asked to create a circuit such that when the switch in the circuit is closed, the light bulb goes from on to off. A simpler form of problem is a circuit modification problem where students are asked to alter a circuit so that its behavior changes. For instance, they could be asked to insert a switch into the circuit so that when the switch is closed, the light will go off. At any point in the circuit construction process, the students can request to see and hear an explanation for the behavior of the circuit that they have created. They must then decide, based upon the behavior of the circuit, whether their design is correct or incorrect.

Creating models of system behavior: Problems in model design, modification, and debugging

In addition to creating and troubleshooting circuits, the learning environment could allow the student to create and debug qualitative models for circuit behavior (the system currently does not have this facility). All of the types of problems that apply to circuit behavior (troubleshooting, prediction, etc.), apply to mental model behavior as well. Thus students could be asked, for example, to locate the buggy device model, or an erroneous circuit principle, or faulty control knowledge contained in a given model (e.g., [3, 5, 35]). In order to determine this, students could present the model with circuits, and observe how it simulates them. Further, they could inspect the model by looking at, for instance, the rules within its device models.

3. Model Evolutions

Most of the work on qualitative modeling within the AI community has been concerned with developing relatively sophisticated models for simulating the behavior of physical phenomena (e.g., see [2]). This is understandable since these researchers are interested in creating intelligent, not naive, machines. However, our interest is in instruction and in possible transitions from novice to expert behavior. We have developed, therefore, simpler zero-order qualitative models for the novice that are easy to learn, that capture important circuit concepts and laws, and that are extendible to more sophisticated ways of reasoning about circuit behavior. Moreover, for purposes of instruction, the zero-order models themselves have been decomposed into a succession of models of increasing complexity, each extending the range of electrical circuit problems that can be understood.

In this section we will characterize the ways in which models can evolve. The major evolutions can be broadly classified using the taxonomy developed in the introduction: (1) an increase in degree of elaboration, (2) order, and (3) a change in perspective. In addition, there are finer grained evolutions that can occur within a model of a particular perspective, order, and degree of elaboration—such as conceptual refinement, generalization, or differentiation. This taxonomy of model evolutions will allow us to create a space of causal model progressions, and will ultimately allow for different learners to pursue alternative paths through the space, depending upon their learning styles and pedagogical goals.

Some of the above model evolutions can involve a change in model form as well as content, that is, a transformation in the way knowledge is represented and applied. For example, when introducing the concept of a fault, one could simply add to each device model rules for altering that device's state variables when the device is faulty. Alternatively, one could introduce general procedures that operate on device models and infer the effects of a fault on the device's state. Another example involves changes in the form of propagation mechanism utilized by the model. One such transformation was given in the previous section, where we described how propagations of changes in voltages could be evaluated: (1) on a device-by-device basis, by tracing backward to the voltage source; or (2) by propagating forward, making voltage redistribution into an explicit process which evaluates the changes in voltages that occur whenever any device changes its state. Another more dramatic transformation in form involves splitting a model into multiple models, such as we have done in creating zero-order models as distinct from first-order models. The fact that causal model progressions can involve transformations in knowledge form as well as content increases the richness of the theory of knowledge evolution—in contrast with, for example, trying to impart knowledge in the form of a collection of independent condition-action rules, such as the set of symptom-fault-fix associations that many experts use in troubleshooting.

3.1. The problem of modifiability

If one's theory of learning involves a concept of model transformations and the view that at each stage in learning the student must develop a runnable model on which to base problem solving, then a primary consideration in designing such evolutionary families of models must be their *modifiability*. Models must be developed with a view towards facilitating their progressive upgrading in response to new problem demands. In this regard, a worthwhile analogy can be made with the programmer's problem of developing code that is maintainable and modifiable. Concepts such as modularity, inheritance, goal decomposition, and the like have evolved within computer science to serve these needs, and they all have their application to the development of progressions of mental models that can be easily learned. For example, to facilitate learning, all devices of a given type should have a common model and that model should be independent of the circuit context in which the device occurs (modularity), and all device models should have a common form (inheritance). Thus, when the concept of a fault state of a device is introduced, it can be easily generalized to other devices.

In considering the learnability of a particular model progression, one must consider not only the concepts and reasoning skills that must be acquired, but also the types of "programming" changes to the student's mental model that the new reasoning would require. These changes can occur to the device models and general circuit principles, as well as to the model's control structure. Each of these types of change poses its own particular problems for the learner who is attempting to modify his or her current model in an appropriate fashion.

Complete rewrites of aspects of the model are likely to be more difficult for the student to achieve than model refinements. However, complete rewrites may sometimes be necessary in order to introduce material in an easily learnable form. For example, the zero-order models enable basic circuit concepts to be acquired more easily than if one started with first-order models. However, the limitations of a zero-order model require the addition of a first-order model, which builds upon the knowledge and structure of the zero-order model, but requires rewrites of many of the zero-order rules.

Consider next the problem of adding knowledge, as when the student learns something entirely new. An example is when transistors are introduced as devices for the first time. In this case, the concept of a device model existed before, but the model for a transistor did not. Adding knowledge is a potentially complex model transformation because one has to decide where to place the knowledge. If the instructional approach involved teaching independent condition-action rules, this would not be an issue. However, in the case of mental models it can be a crucial issue. For instance, does one place a new rule or concept in the prototypical device model so that all other device models inherit the knowledge, or does it belong in the device model for, say, a transistor? Even further, it is possible that the rule is a general principle of circuit behavior and does not belong in a device model at all. Considerations of where a particular piece of knowledge should be embedded in the students' mental model are important in determining the learnability and useability of the model.

A final example of a model transformation that may cause difficulty in learning is the alteration of the control knowledge that students employ to manage their reasoning about circuit behavior. For example, at the beginning of instruction, students may be asked to reason about the behavior of only one device within a circuit, such as a light bulb. For such problems, the student's model needs only to activate one device model plus the basic circuit principles that are needed to determine the behavior of the device within the circuit. However, later in the progression students are asked to reason about multiple devices within a circuit. Initially this can be done serially, but as soon as devices such as capacitors and transistors are introduced, it must be done "in parallel" or, alternatively, one must introduce the voltage redistribution process. Thus, the form of the student's model gets more complex in that control procedures that were initially unnecessary, or at least were very simple, must now increase in complexity. Similar kinds of control complexities are introduced when students go from troubleshooting just opens, or just shorts to ground, to attempting to locate either type of fault within a circuit. Moreover, for purposes of economy in reasoning, students may wish to retain multiple control structures so that they can reason using the simpler control structure when a problem allows it. There is thus the added complexity of learning the contexts in which a particular control structure is applicable.

Finally, it should be noted that the type of model transformation can also affect the ease or difficulty a student has in *using* the model to reason about circuits. For instance, changes that increase the complexity of the model's control structure could make the model not only more difficult to learn but more difficult to use as well. Creating model progressions must take into account not only models' modifiability, but also how easily they can be put into practice in solving problems.

3.2. Types of micromodel evolutions

This section will discuss the types of "micro" evolutions that can occur within a model of a particular perspective, order, and degree of elaboration, such as evolutions that could occur within the zero-order, behavioral models. In learning, a model's knowledge may be augmented by refining, generalizing, or differentiating an existing knowledge component, by adding or substituting a new component, or by integrating several existing components within some larger conceptual framework. Each of these transformations represents a type of knowledge evolution and a possible pedagogical goal for the student to pursue. The following are examples of each of these ways in which a student could choose to progress, presented in the order of a possible knowledge evolution:

(1) *Knowledge acquisition*. The student acquires a new concept or law or problem-solving skill. For example, many novices, as we have discussed, need to acquire the basic concepts of conductivity, circuit, and voltage drop.

(2) *Knowledge differentiation*. The student learns how an existing concept can be differentiated into two concepts. For instance, once students have acquired the concept of conductivity, they learn that it can be differentiated into conductive-resistive (i.e., a resistance) and purely conductive.

(3) *Knowledge integration*. The student integrates two concepts. For example, students need to synthesize their new concept of purely conductive paths with their concept of voltage drop—purely conductive devices do not have voltage drops across them and any device connected directly across such a purely conductive device cannot have a voltage drop across it.

(4) *Knowledge generalization*. The student learns how an existing concept applies in a wide range of contexts. For example, students could generalize this new concept of a purely conductive parallel path (i.e., a short) from being immediately across a device to being anywhere on the device's feed path to any point on its return path or even immediately to ground (i.e., a short to ground). Also, students could learn that their new concept of resistance acquired in the context of a resistor can also be applied to other devices, such as light bulb or the collector-emitter path of a transistor.

(5) *Knowledge refinement*. The student refines an existing concept. For example, students can refine their understanding of voltage drop by observing that in parallel circuits, a device only needs for one of its feed paths to be "unshorted" in order to have a voltage applied to it.

(6) *Knowledge substitution*. The student replaces an earlier concept or skill with another. For example, students may go on to substitute causal propagation based upon voltage redistributions for the device-by-device tracing of feed and ground paths. Note that substitutions can be regarded as reversible (as in this example) or nonreversible.

Students may differ in the type of evolution they prefer at different stages of learning. One student may prefer, for example, to generalize first and differentiate later, whereas another may prefer to differentiate first and generalize later. The selection of appropriate model transformation goals during learning involves a consideration of not only students' learning styles and the difficulty of the transformation, but also the purposes for which they are learning about circuit behavior. If, for example, students are learning for the purposes of acquiring skill in troubleshooting circuits, the path through the model progression space that is most appropriate may be different from that for students who have the goal of designing circuits.

At any point in learning, different types of model transformations are possible that increase the sophistication of the model's reasoning in different ways. A particular path through the space of possible model progressions embodies one possible transition from novice to expert status. Our ultimate goal is to create a space of possible model progressions and to add facilities to the learning environment that will help students to select a path through this model space based upon their own pedagogical styles and goals. Within the present project, we have focused on tutoring troubleshooting, and have constrained the network of possible model evolutions to a linear progression, i.e., a curriculum. The curriculum has the objective of teaching troubleshooting for opens and shorts to ground in series-parallel circuits using the zero-order circuit model and the approach to troubleshooting described in the previous section. We have evaluated our implementation of this curriculum within the QUEST system using a small group of high-school students, and have found the tutoring approach to be effective. This work is described in more depth by White and Frederiksen [47, 49], as well as in Section 4.2.

3.3. Evolutions in model order and degree of elaboration

In addition to the "fine-gained" progressions that can occur in the development of a particular model, "larger-grained" progressions also occur, characterized by changes in model order and degree of elaboration.[13] In the following, we will illustrate how, in developing behavioral models of circuits, transitions from qualitative to quantitative models might be interleaved with increases in the degree of model elaboration. In this discussion, two levels of model elaboration will be distinguished, one in which the circuit principles included allow the student to reason about voltage distributions within a circuit, and a second in which additional principles are added to incorporate reasoning about current flow within the circuit. To help illustrate the progression, the reasoning of these different models will be presented for two simple transistor circuits (shown in Figs. 7 and 8).

3.3.1. The initial degree of elaboration: Reasoning about voltages

Zero-order model
In the initial, zero-order model (described more fully in the previous sections), students are introduced to the basic idea of a circuit. In this context, they learn that there are two polarities of electrical force, and that for an electrical force to be applied to a device (such as a light bulb), both polarities must be applied, respectively, to two ports of the device. They also learn that devices have properties such as being a source of voltage (e.g., batteries) or not, and being conductive (e.g., bulbs and wires) or nonconductive (e.g., open switches). Finally, they learn that devices can have more than one state (e.g., a switch can be open or closed), and that the state can determine the device's properties (e.g., nonconductive or conductive). Experience with circuit problems leads then to a general idea of a series circuit: it must contain one or more voltage sources, and all elements in it must be conductive for there to be a voltage across all of its components—if a single device within the circuit is nonconductive, then that device will have a voltage applied to it and no other device will have a voltage drop across it. Thus, students develop knowledge of where

---

[13] The only models that are at present implemented in our prototype learning environment are the zero-order models, at the level of elaboration described in Section 2.

voltage drops will be present in a series circuit containing conductive and nonconductive components.

Next, students are presented with a more sophisticated model that knows about series-parallel circuits and can introduce the concept of a short, i.e., a purely conductive path that eliminates voltage drops across components connected in parallel with it. This particular model transformation can be motivated by giving students problems where they have to predict, for instance, the behavior of the light bulb in the circuit shown in Fig. 2 as the switch is opened and closed. In this model progression, students must differentiate their concept of a conductive path into conductive-resistive and purely conductive paths. Thus, their concept of conductivity must be refined and this refinement must be integrated into their voltage concept—the concept must now incorporate the fact that if there is a purely conductive path immediately across a device, then no voltage is applied to that device.

Then, using a light bulb as a fledgling voltmeter, students learn that the distribution of voltages within a series-parallel circuit follows a zero-order version of Kirchhoff's Voltage Law: there is no voltage drop across purely conductive components (which can include parallel subcircuits) within a series circuit, and there is a voltage drop across all resistive elements (provided that the circuit contains no nonconductive elements). Using this zero-order model, students learn how changes in conductivity of components can alter the distribution of voltages in the circuit, and thereby cause other devices to change their state (for example, a transistor may go from the unsaturated to the saturated state). Students first learn to evaluate the effects of changes in conductivity on a device-by-device basis, and then they learn principles for redistributing voltages as an alternative technique for carrying out propagations.

Students learn to apply this knowledge in troubleshooting, in carrying out circuit design problems, and in predicting the behavior of circuits. For example, one could apply the zero-order model to reason about the behavior of a transistor amplifier such as the common-emitter amplifier shown in Fig. 7. This requires a device model for the npn transistor which employs the following rules:

Transistor

States: Saturated or Unsaturated.

If the base-emitter (B-E) voltage of the transistor is positive, then it is in the saturated state; otherwise, it is in the unsaturated state.

Internal Conductivity:

If the state is unsaturated, then the collector-emitter (C-E) is nonconductive.

If the state is saturated, then the C-E is purely conductive.

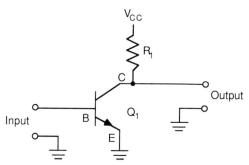

Fig. 7. A simple common-emitter amplifier. (V_{CC} stands for the positive side of the voltage source.)

These rules treat the transistor as a switch that is controlled by the voltage applied to the base-emitter. Applying this model to the common-emitter amplifier, when the input voltage to the amplifier is positive, the C-E of Q_1 will be purely conductive, creating a short across the output, which causes the output voltage to be zero. When the input voltage is zero, the C-E of transistor Q_1 is nonconductive, and there is then a good feed path from the positive side of the output to V_{CC} (the positive terminal of the battery) through R_1. The voltage across the output is therefore positive. Thus, the zero-order model allows one to discover that the amplifier inverts the input signal (high in, low out, and vice versa). The common-emitter amplifier could actually be used in this way within digital circuits as long as the input voltage is switched to high enough levels to ensure that the transistor becomes fully saturated.

The first-order model
Within a first-order model, students generalize the zero-order concepts to reason about the effects of incremental changes. For example, students learn that reducing the resistance of a component within a series circuit causes a drop in the voltage across that component (the R→V Rule[14]) and an increase in voltage across the other components in the circuit (Kirchhoff's Voltage Law or KVL). Thus they learn how incremental changes in resistance and voltage influence, in an incremental manner, the distribution of voltages within a circuit, and how these changes in voltage can cause devices within the circuit to incrementally change their state variables in a sequence of causal propagations.

    Students could apply these principles widely. For example, in simple ana-logue circuits, they could develop an understanding of how a simple amplifier works, such as the common-emitter amplifier shown in Fig. 7. In first-order models, the transistor is modeled as increasing in conductivity across the

---

[14] The R→V Rule states that a decrease in the resistance of a component causes a decrease in the voltage across the component, except if the component is directly connected to a constant voltage source.

collector-emitter (C-E) pathway whenever there is an increase in the base-emitter (B-E) voltage, and as decreasing in C-E conductivity (or, alternatively, increasing in resistance) when the B-E voltage decreases.[15] In the common-emitter amplifier, an increase in the B-E voltage of the transistor (the input signal) causes an increase in the conductivity of the C-E circuit of the transistor (as specified in the first-order model of a transistor). This in turn causes the voltage across C-E to decrease (the R→V Rule), which is the output voltage of the amplifier. Thus, an important characteristic of the common-emitter amplifier can be deduced: changes in the output voltage of the amplifier will be the mirror image of changes in the imput voltage (i.e., the output will be 180 degrees out of phase with the input).

Reasoning such as this can also be applied by students in understanding such circuit concepts as feedback [47]. For example, consider the common-collector amplifier shown in Fig. 8. In this amplifier, an increase in the input voltage causes an increase in the B-E voltage of transistor Q_1 (using KVL applied to the loop consisting of the input voltage source, the B-E of Q_1, and R_2). Applying the device model for the transistor, the conductivity of the C-E of Q_1 increases, and the voltage across C-E decreases (by the R→V Rule). Since the voltage across R_2 must therefore increase (by KVL for the loop containing the voltage source, C-E of Q_1, and R_2), the output voltage increases. However, in this amplifier there is negative feedback. Since the voltage across R_2 increased, the voltage across B-E of Q_1 must *decrease* (by KVL applied to the loop made up of the input voltage source, now assumed to be fixed, the B-E of Q_1, and R_2). Thus, the feedback is a voltage in the opposite polarity to the initial increment in the input voltage, and this implies that the feedback is negative.[16] First-order models are essential for detecting and understanding feedback, as de Kleer [14] has argued.[17]

The quantitative model
In the quantitative model, Kirchhoff's Voltage Law is generalized to its quantitative form: the sum of voltages in any loop is zero. Students are

---

[15] Increases in conductivity of the C-E of course correspond to increases in the C-E current through the transistor. Modeling the transistor with a direct causal link between B-E voltage and C-E current is reserved for models at the second degree of elaboration (see below).

[16] If one continued the propagation sequence, the amplifier would be found to cycle endlessly between increasing the output voltage and decreasing it. Such repeating cycles within a qualitative theory correspond to continuous processes in a quantitative theory [44], and the student needs to learn to recognize them as such.

[17] A zero-order analysis of the common-collector amplifier simply shows the transistor switching from the unsaturated state (for a zero input voltage) to the saturated state (for a positive input voltage), with the output going from zero to positive. This is, in fact, an accurate portrayal of the gross behavior of the amplifier, since the feedback can never completely cancel the input. (Rather, it has the function of increasing the input impedance.) Within first-order models, reasoning about the relative magnitudes of input and feedback signals involves importing external knowledge that is not contained in the qualitative models themselves.

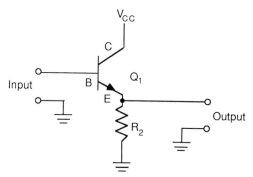

Fig. 8. A simple common-collector amplifier. (V_{CC} stands for the positive side of the voltage source.)

introduced to the concept of a voltage divider (a set of resistive devices in series, connected across a voltage source), and shown that the total voltage across the divider is given by the sum of the voltage drops across the individual resistive devices, and that the magnitude of each individual voltage drop is proportional to the resistance of that device relative to the total resistance in the circuit. Thus, quantitative laws can be presented as model extensions that are useful when quantitative problems are encountered. They are not presented as a substitute for qualitative models, or even as more desirable or more correct. Indeed, students by this point would already have appreciated the importance of qualitative models in inferring the behavior of a complex circuit such as a digital logic circuit, in troubleshooting, and in circuit design.

3.3.2. *The second degree of elaboration*: *Reasoning about current flow*

Zero-order model
Within the zero-order models, current is initially defined locally for each device (Ohm's Law). Whenever a voltage is applied to a conductive device, current will flow through the device in the direction of the negative source of voltage.[18] When no voltage is applied to a device, no current flows. Furthermore, if a device is nonconductive, no current can flow through it; and if it is purely conductive, it offers no resistance to a current flow. These rules allow students to derive current flow locally after using voltage distribution laws to assign voltages throughout the circuit. For example, suppose that a light bulb were connected across the output of the common-collector amplifier of Fig. 8. Applying the zero-order model for redistributing voltages within the amplifier allowed us to deduce that when the input voltage is positive, there is a voltage applied to the light bulb (the output). If we now apply the local rule for determining current (Ohm's Law), we can conclude that a current will flow

---

[18] This is the usual convention, which refers to the flow of positive charge.

through the light bulb. Similarly, when the input voltage is zero, there will be no voltage applied to the light bulb and therefore no current flow through it. The same reasoning can be applied to derive currents through the other components in the circuit.

After they are acquainted with the local application of Ohm's Law for determining current flow, students would then be introduced to additional principles for reasoning about current flow within a circuit. In particular, they would be presented with a model which incorporates Kirchhoff's Current Law (KCL). This law states that (1) the current flowing into a device will equal that flowing out of a device, and (2) if there is a current flowing out of a port of a device, there will be a current flowing into any device(s) connected to that device port. In addition, they learn to apply Ohm's Law (relating resistance to current flow) to reason about current flow within parallel circuits: If one branch of a parallel circuit contains no resistance, then all of the current flowing into the parallel circuit will flow through the purely conductive branch and no current will flow through the resistive branch.

As well as the introduction of these circuit principles, revisions are also made to device models for devices such as the transistor: In addition to a rule relating the B-E voltage to the conductivity of the C-E, a new rule would be added allowing a direct inference to be made about the C-E current—when a positive voltage is applied to the B-E, there will be a current through the C-E (otherwise, there is no C-E current). With these new principles, students would now have an alternate way of reasoning about current flow within series and parallel circuits, which provides an alternative means for deriving the current flow through components (in addition to using voltage propagations and the local rule for current flow). For example, we shall apply this alternative model to analyze current flow in the common-collector amplifier discussed above (given in Fig. 8). When the input voltage applied to the amplifier is positive, the C-E of Q_1 will have a current through it (by the revised transistor model). Then, applying KCL, if there is a current flowing out of the emitter of Q_1, there will be a current flowing into both R_2 and the light bulb, which is connected across the output (since both offer paths towards the negative side of the voltage source). Thus, using KCL provides an alternate way to propagate the effect of an input voltage on current flow through the light bulb. In this way, students would have a first experience with a model which contains redundancies and that allows alternative correct solutions to a circuit problem.

First-order model

In this model, increasing the voltage applied to a device having a fixed resistance causes an increase in current through the device (Ohm's Law). Likewise, when the voltage across a device is fixed, decreasing its resistance will cause there to be an increase in current through the device (also Ohm's Law). Finally, for a fixed resistance, increases in the current through a device can be inferred to have been brought about by an increase in the voltage across the device (this is presented as a form of backwards reasoning using Ohm's Law). Since in first-order models variables such as resistance, voltage, and current have qualitative derivatives (rather than being regarded merely as present or absent as in the zero-order models), Kirchhoff's Current Law (KCL) can be restated: (1) for any component, increasing the current flowing into the component results in an increase in that flowing out of the component, and (2) increasing the current flowing into a node (or point where two or more components are connected) will result in an increase in that flowing out of the node. With these additional principles, students could learn to reason directly about changes in current in both series and parallel circuits.

In the first-order model, a further revision is made to the transistor model to relate increments (decrements) in B-E voltage to increases (decreases) in the C-E current. This revision then allows alternative propagations in modeling the operation of transistor circuits. For example, for the common-emitter amplifier previously discussed (see Fig. 7), increasing the input voltage (across B-E of Q_1) causes an increase in the current through the C-E of Q_1 (by the transistor model), which causes an increase in the current through R_1 (by KCL). Since the resistance of R_1 is fixed, we can use Ohm's Law to infer that the voltage across R_1 must have increased. Finally, since the voltage across R_1 increased, that across C-E of Q_1 (which is the output) must have decreased (by applying KVL to the loop made up of R_1, C-E of Q_1, and the voltage source). Reasoning such as this is very much in the spirit of that of de Kleer [14]. We should also note that other propagations for the behavior of such circuits are possible using the set of constraints offered by the qualitative forms of Ohm's Law, Kirchhoff's Voltage and Current Laws, and the alternative rules within the device models. Thus, students will learn that the behavior of a physical system can be envisioned in more than one way, due to redundancies in the set of circuit principles that are used for deducing the system's behavior.

Quantitative circuit theory
The quantitative relations between voltage and current, and between resistance and current, are initially introduced as proportionalities: e.g., when the resistance is fixed, the current is directly proportional to voltage. Kirchhoff's Current Law is restated as: The sum of currents leaving any node of a circuit equals that entering the node (i.e., there is conservation of charge). By introducing a series of problems and their qualitative and quantitative analyses, and by collecting data from circuits used in these problems, students would derive for themselves a number of laws, such as Ohm's Law and the formula for the resistance of resistors connected in parallel. The quantitative theory is thus presented simply as an extension of the qualitative theory, but one which allows algebraic equations for expressing the underlying circuit principles (which by now should be quite familiar to the student). Students would also

learn that problems can be solved through the algebraic manipulation of equations, but that each manipulation is based on circuit concepts that can be thought about in qualitative terms. Students should also discover that there are many classes of problems that are not amenable to such quantitative solutions, such as reasoning about the behavior of circuits, troubleshooting, or circuit design. In most cases, the quantitative model serves as a useful adjunct to qualitative reasoning in solving problems rather than as a replacement for it.

Summary
This progression of models increasing in order and degree of elaboration should enable students to develop multiple models of circuit behavior. Reasoning about a circuit in multiple ways allows for different conceptualizations that in turn serve different purposes. For example, zero-order models facilitate reasoning about gross circuit behavior, and can be used in studying the behavior of digital circuits and their functionality. They can also be used in analyzing extreme cases when one is studying the behavior of analogue circuits such as the amplifier circuits. First-order models are useful in studying analogue circuits, and can explain feedback, or how such circuits respond to changes in input voltages. Furthermore, they can serve as a bridge to reasoning using quantitative models. Quantitative models can explain such features of circuit behavior as thresholds, can provide the reason certain components are present within a circuit (such as current limiting resistors), and can of course be used to calculate actual voltages and currents within a circuit. An important problem for future research is the model selection problem: how do experts invoke appropriate conceptualizations for a particular problem at hand, and how can students be taught how to select and coordinate multiple models in problem solving.

3.4. Developing alternative perspectives

The model evolutions discussed so far have been with respect to the students' behavioral models of circuit operation. However, just because students are adept at looking at circuit diagrams and predicting circuit behavior does not mean that they have a "deep" understanding of electrical circuits. They may be completely unable to describe the *functionality* of circuits—the purpose of a circuit as a whole and the role that subsets of devices play in achieving that purpose. Also, they may understand nothing about the *underlying physics of device and circuit functioning*. For instance, they may be unable to answer questions of the form: "Why does the collector current of a transistor depend upon the base-emitter voltage?" and "Why are voltage drops within a series circuit proportional to resistances?" Thus we argue that in order to attain a "deep understanding" of how a circuit works, students must evolve such alternative conceptualizations of circuit phenomena and be able to apply them in conjunction with their models of circuit behavior.

3.4.1. *Functional models*

We have explored two approaches to developing in students a means for mapping from their qualitative models of circuit behavior to a functional understanding of circuits. Both approaches are based upon a study of the behavior of components of a circuit, and how their behavior depends upon the behavior of other components within the circuit. In each approach, the function of a circuit emerges from a study of its behavior as inputs to the circuit are allowed to vary. The two approaches differ in the nature of the components that are the focus of study: In the first approach, the focus is on devices within the circuit that have multiple states, while in the second, it is on designated subcircuits that constitute functional units in the design of the circuit.

The first approach adopts a *device focus* and emphasizes the discovery of patterns of interdependence among devices within a circuit. To facilitate this, students are shown how to construct a representation of the dependencies among devices within a circuit. For example, in a simple circuit, the state of one transistor may depend upon the states of two other transistors in the circuit. Suppose further that when the first two transistors are both saturated (e.g., "on"), the dependent transistor is also "on," while if either of them is unsaturated ("off"), the dependent transistor remains "off." Device inter-dependencies such as this one can be represented in a state dependency graph whose nodes represent devices and whose links represent particular dependencies. In the present example, the third transistor would be linked to the other two. By further parsing this dependency graph, sets of links and nodes performing specific functions (in the example, a logic gate) can be identified, and an analysis of the circuit as a set of interconnected functional units can be performed [47]. In the present case, three transistors are acting as an AND gate and the inputs to the first two transistors are providing inputs to that gate. In this way, circuit functions emerge from a study of the behavior of devices within the circuit. The implementation of these functions within the circuit can be seen by looking back to the specifics of the causal propagations that generated the specific functional dependencies at issue.[19]

The second approach to constructing a link between behavioral and functional models focuses on a study of the input-output relations for designated *"chunks"* of a circuit. In this approach, interesting circuit chunks (or subcircuits) are presented to the student, and the student's task is to discover the

---

[19] The alternative of basing the functional analysis on the causal trace which results from applying the behavioral model to the circuit, as de Kleer [14] has advocated, has the disadvantage that the causal derivations of circuit behavior are not unique, and depend as we have seen on the particular qualitative constraints one has chosen to employ in explaining circuit behavior. For example, classifying the function of a resistor as either a "current-to-voltage converter" or a "voltage divider" depends upon the particular circuit laws used in deriving the circuit's behavior. Basing the functional classification on such causal derivations thus leads to ambiguous classifications.

function performed by the particular subcircuit. The subcircuits chosen are the functional units circuit designers use in building more complex circuits.[20] For such interesting subcircuits (e.g., the common-collector and common-emitter amplifiers in Figs. 7 and 8), the student explores the outputs that occur for each of the possible inputs they may receive in a larger circuit context. To illustrate, if the context is that of digital logic circuits, students would employ zero-order models and analyze the behavior of the amplifiers for cases where the input voltages are either high or zero They would then discover the function performed by each—the common-emitter amplifier would be seen to act as an inverter, while the common-collector amplifier would simply pass through the input logic value. If on the other hand the context is an analogue circuit, students would need to use first-order (and quantitative) models to understand the functionality of the amplifiers. Thus, the form of qualitative model applied depends upon the context in which the subcircuit occurs. The analysis of circuit function is based on its input-output relations viewed from the perspective of a model of a particular order, and not on the specific steps of the causal propagation employed in deriving its behavior.

Once students have understood the functions of subcircuits, they then learn to model the behavior of larger circuits composed of these subcircuits. They are introduced to a new (and simple) way to analyze the interactions among such components, viewing each as a receiver and transmitter of information. Information received by a circuit component (the set of input signals) is processed (for example, the logical operation AND is performed, or an input signal is inverted), and an output signal is then created and sent on to other components. This simple information-processing model for simulating the functional behavior of large circuits is similar to that used by experts, and can be used as a basis for tutoring troubleshooting [25].

3.4.2. Reductionistic, physical models

Explanations of circuit behavior rely on qualitative models of devices and on general circuit principles which incorporate the basic laws of circuit theory relating voltage, resistance, and current. However, neither the device models nor the circuit principles are explicitly derived for the student from more elementary physical principles; rather, they are simply represented as rules that are applicable to circuits in general. To foster a deeper understanding, it is possible to develop coherent models for devices and explanations of the basic steady state circuit principles in terms of a more elementary physical theory. In

---

[20] Circuit designers do not create circuits "bottom up"; rather, they implement a top-level function using a repertoire of subcircuits having known functions, which are realized by the behavioral interaction of their subcomponents. For this reason, one can argue that while the student should understand the way in which the subcircuits implement their functions and how such subcircuits together implement top-level functions, they do not need to learn how to discover functionally significant subcircuits within a larger circuit context.

this theory, electrical forces within a circuit are derived from, and in turn influence, the distributions of charged particles within the components of a circuit. Such physical models are quite commonplace in introductory textbooks, where they are used to explain the behavior of devices such as capacitors, diodes, and transistors. What is lacking, however, is a bridge from the physics of electrically charged particles (e.g., Coulomb's Law) and mechanics (e.g., Newton's Laws) to an understanding of the basic circuit laws (e.g., Ohm's and Kirchhoff's Laws) that form the backbone of circuit theory.

We are working on a simple, physical model that focuses on the electrical fields that exist when there are nonuniform distributions of positive and negative charge carriers within a circuit.[21] For example, a battery produces an excess of positive charge carriers on one terminal and an excess of negative charge carriers on the other. An electrical field thus exists around each battery terminal. These electrical fields can act upon any mobile charge carriers that are within adjacent regions,[22] attracting those with a like charge and repelling those with an unlike charge. This movement of charge carriers in turn alters their distribution within adjacent regions of a circuit, which then induces additional migrations of charge carriers, and so forth. This simplified physical model can explain how within a circuit a voltage drop develops across a resistor (a device which, within the model, slows down or impedes the movement of charge carriers), and how a constant current is developed within a circuit containing a voltage source. Moreover, applying the model to simple series and parallel circuits can reveal the mechanisms underlying circuit principles such as Kirchhoff's and Ohm's Laws. These principles become emergent properties of such circuits, representing the behavior of charge carriers when the physical model has reached a steady state. For example, one can illustrate how in a series circuit containing a nonconductive element, the entire voltage drop develops across that element. Furthermore, it is possible to show how, when the nonconductive element (e.g., a switch) becomes conductive, the voltages are redistributed across resistive elements of the circuit. Depending upon the form of measurements that are taken during the operation of the physical model and the circuit problems to which it is applied, the model can be used to emphasize particular circuit principles (involving voltage or current) such as are introduced within the progression of behavioral models, in either their qualitative (zero- or first-order) or quantitative forms. The particular circuit principles emphasized can be chosen to be compatible with the order and degree of elaboration of the behavioral model currently being developed. We

---

[21] Haertel has developed a similar type of model, although it differs in certain key respects from ours (see [24, 29]).

[22] Coulomb's Law, of course, states that the force between charged particles decreases with the square of the distance; however, within the qualitative physical model, we limit the influence of an electrical charge to an adjacent "region," beyond which it has no direct influence. Thus, we allow action only at "near" distances.

hypothesize that linking the behavioral models to students' intuitive notions of "attractive pulls" and "repulsive pushes" via the introduction of this reductionistic, physical model will increase the learnability of the behavioral model, as well as improve the depth of the students' understanding.

A physical model such as this, when implemented, will allow the student to request a change in perspective from macroscopic to microscopic models of circuit behavior. The microscopic model will be able to explain and simulate the causality of circuit operation in terms of electrical forces and their effects on the behavior of charge carriers within the circuit. These explanations will be consistent with the voltage redistribution process of the macroscopic models, and the macroscopic circuit principles will emerge from the operation of the microscopic model.

3.5. Coordinating multiple models

This paper has addressed issues relating to the learnability of a set of mental models. In discussing learnability, our primary construct was that of *causal consistency*. The construct applies to the relationship among models of differing orders and degrees of elaboration. For instance, we argued that electric force should be the causal agent within both qualitative and quantitative models of circuit behavior; and we argued further that when these models are elaborated to incorporate principles for reasoning about changes in current, that these changes should be explained in terms of electric force. The construct of causal consistency also applies across models of different perspectives. For instance, we stated that our objective in creating microscopic models of circuit behavior was to enable the principles governing our macroscopic models (such as KVL) to become emergent properties of the microscopic models, and similarly we illustrated (in [47]) how the principles governing circuit functioning can emerge from the types of causal models of circuit behavior described in this paper. Thus we argue that causal consistency across domain models of differing perspective, order, and degree of elaboration can increase the learnability of the set of mental models that are necessary to "deeply" understand domain phenomena.

We can also apply similar arguments to define the properties that this set of mental models must possess in order to enable them to play a role in helping students to understand the phenomena of other domains. For example, can acquiring this set of electrical circuit models facilitate learning the concepts, laws, and models needed to understand other physical systems? The answer to this question depends upon the *causal generality* of the concepts and laws embedded in the models. For example, if the models of microscopic circuit behavior are based upon concepts such as force, acceleration, and equilibrium (which we are attempting to do), then the acquisition of such a model can foster and be fostered by an understanding of mechanics. Similarly, if one's models of circuit functionality are based upon general principles of information flow, the acquisition of such a model can foster and be fostered by an understanding of computer science. The thesis is that understanding and learning are facilitated by a consistency of concepts and causal relations across different types of models and across different domains. This paper has attempted to show that such consistency is possible. The view is compatible with the "generality hypothesis" that governs much AI research, as well as research on physical theories (both qualitative and quantitative).

4. The Learning Environment

We have focused on creating a progression of models that makes a gradual transition from naivete to expertise. To facilitate this transition, the instructional system:

(1) emphasizes a qualitative, causal analysis that builds upon novices' existing knowledge;

(2) motivates learning via problem solving and appropriate problem selections; and

(3) generates causal explanations of circuit behavior, and illustrates problem-solving strategies.

The assumption is that (1) by giving students problems that present a manageable cognitive challenge (that is, problems they could solve with a small revision to their mental model) and are inherently interesting (such as troubleshooting or circuit prediction problems), and (2) by presenting students with examples of model reasoning via verbal and visual descriptions of circuit behavior, students will, at any stage in the learning process, be able to transform their model to match that of the system. Our view is that incorrect inductions are not a necessary consequence of the learning process. The hypothesis is that in learning environments where the model progression and problem sets are designed appropriately, incorrect model transformations are unlikely. The tutoring system therefore does not actively attempt to diagnose and treat wrong model transformations. It does, however, provide feedback, and it allows the student to compare his or her reasoning with that of the model that is currently driving the system. Juxtaposing the student's and system's problem solving allows the student to debug his or her model when difficulty is encountered.

The progression of models is used to define problem sets that motivate transformations in the student's mental model. At any stage in learning, the instructional goal of the student is to master the model that is currently driving the simulation environment. The method of bringing about such a transformation is to instantiate it in problems for the student to work out. The instructional system presents to the student those problems that can be solved under the transformed model but not under the untransformed model. The students are thus motivated to revise their current model. The theory is that, by giving students problems in this set (i.e., problems that are just beyond their level of competence), students will be motivated to revise their model. This model revision will be facilitated because it requires only a small change to their present model, in an environment where feedback and explanations are available to help them understand the model transformation. Moreover, the models have been designed with the requirement of modifiability in mind. Students should thus be motivated and able to transform their model into the next model in the sequence.[23]

The initial sequence of problems in each set is crucial to facilitating a correct model transformation. In particular, the initial problems need to be selected so that they can be solved by the transformed model but not by some other erroneous model transformation. This helps to avoid the induction of "buggy" mental models. After the correct model transformation has been induced, the remaining problems serve the function of giving students practice in using their new mental model of circuit behavior.

Model progressions also determine the focus of explanations. To facilitate model transformations, the system can turn any problem into an example for the student by reasoning out loud while it solves the problem, focusing its explanations on the difference between the transformed and the untransformed model. The difference between models also defines what aspects of reasoning should be represented graphically to the student. For instance, if students are learning about determining when there is or is not a voltage drop across a device, the system illustrates paths to voltage sources. However, later in the model progression, when it is assumed that students already know how to determine the presence of a voltage drop, the paths are no longer displayed.

In summary, the particular model transformation undertaken at each stage in the progression of models enables one to determine (1) what problems to present to the student, (2) what aspects of circuit behavior to articulate verbally, and (3) what aspects of circuit behavior and of the problem-solving process to visually display to the student.

4.1. Interacting with the learning environment

Basing the system on a progression of qualitative models makes it possible for students to have considerable freedom in determining the way they interact

---

[23] In addition to problems requiring the transformed model, some problems need to be interspersed from the previous problem set, in order to provide negative exemplars of a concept. For example, if students were learning that a short from a point on a device's feed path to a point on its ground path prevents the device from having a voltage drop across it, and if all the problems were cases of this sort (i.e., where there was always a short from feed to ground), then students would never see negative instances (i.e., cases where there was no short). As Bruner, Goodnow, and Austin [6] have demonstrated, negative instances of a concept are very important to learning. Providing some problems from the previous set can serve this function.

with the learning environment. Students can choose whether to advance to new levels in the progression or to review earlier problems. They can attempt to solve problems on their own, or can request the tutor to give demonstrations and explanations. They can use a circuit editor to alter existing problems or create new circuits, and can add or remove faults from a circuit they have been given or one they have created. The system supports this wide range of activities by being able to simulate the behavior of a circuit that is constructed and by providing explanations of its operation.

All of these functions of the instructional system are provided, at a given point in the learning progression, by the model that is currently driving the learning environment. Each model can:

(1) *Simulate circuit behavior.* A given model is able to accurately simulate the behavior of a certain class of circuits. (The models can, in fact, simulate the behavior of any circuit, however, the simulation will not be accurate for all circuits.)

(2) *Tutor the students.* By reasoning out loud, the model can generate qualitative, causal explanations for circuit behavior.

(3) *Model the students.* The students are assumed to have the current model when they can correctly solve problems that the current model can solve but the previous model could not.

Each model can thus serve as a circuit simulator, a tutor, and a student model.

This architecture for an intelligent learning environment allows students great flexibility in their choice of an instructional strategy. Particular strategies they might use include the following:

– *Exploration and discovery learning.* Students can construct circuits, explore their behavior (by changing the states of devices, inserting faults, and adding or deleting components), and request explanations for the observed behaviors. Students can thus create their own problems and experiment with circuits. The system thereby permits an open-ended exploratory learning strategy.

– *Learning via induction and feedback.* In addition, the progression of models enables the system to present students with a sequence of problem-solving situations that motivate the need for developing particular transformations of their models of circuit behavior. In solving new problems, the students attempt to transform their models of circuit behavior in concordance with the evolution of the system's models. The focus is on having students solve problems on their own, without providing them first with explanations for how to solve them—they are just given feedback as to whether their answers are right or wrong and have to induce the model transformation for themselves.

– *Learning from examples and explanations.* Alternatively, students can be presented with tutorial demonstrations for solving example problems by simply asking the system to reason out loud about a given circuit using its present qualitative, causal model. Students can thus hear explanations of how to solve each type of problem in the series, followed by opportunities to solve similar problems. This strategy thus focuses on presenting examples together with explanations prior to practice in problem solving.

  – *Mixed strategies*. Students can of course also use mixed learning strategies. For example, they can combine inductive learning with the use of examples and explanations. They can also use the circuit editor to modify and experiment with problems presented to them by the system.

  The tutoring system also provides students with additional tools to help them direct their own learning. The concept of a progression of models allows students to understand which models have been mastered and which remain to be learned. They are provided with a map of the learning space that is defined by the progression. This provides students with information about the instructional objective of each model. The students can use this map to select topics of study and to access the associated problem sets.

  The systems's capabilities of allowing different learning strategies and providing tools for self-directed learning are important from several respects. First, they allow for individual differences in learning style—not all students learn best using the same pedagogical technique [11]. Second, they provide students with a sense of autonomy that may be a crucial factor in motivation. Finally, we argue that experiences in managing their own learning, in an environment that makes explicit the evolution of domain knowledge and the possible pedagogical strategies, should play a valuable role in helping students to develop the skills that are needed to become expert learners.

4.2. Instructional effectiveness

The learning environment was tried out on seven high-school students who had had no formal instruction in circuit theory. (The results are further described and discussed in [47].) The students were initially shown a demonstration of how to use the various facilities of the system and then given the opportunity to use those facilities to control the functions of the system while learning. Thus, the students could browse through the topics in the curriculum (as embedded in the progression of qualitative models), select problem sets to try, decide for themselves when to go on to a new topic (i.e., a more sophisticated model), and could use the circuit editor to alter a given circuit. In addition, whenever they so desired, they could ask the associated circuit model to simulate the circuit's behavior and to articulate its reasoning. They could also point to any device in the circuit and ask for an explanation as to why the device was in a particular state. Similarly, they could ask the troubleshooting algorithm resident at that state in the progression to demonstrate and explain how it would locate a fault in the circuit.

The students were given a set of circuit problems as a pre-test, and asked to explain the behavior of each circuit as the states of devices within it were manipulated. As described earlier in the paper, the students initially exhibited serious misconceptions about circuit behavior and lacked key electrical concepts. Further, none of them had had any experience with troubleshooting. The students then spent from five to six days, an hour a day, working with the system. The students were then given the same six circuit problems they had attempted in the pre-test along with three troubleshooting problems, and were asked to explain the behavior of the circuit or to troubleshoot.

After five hours of working within the learning environment on an individual basis, all seven of the students were able to make accurate model-based predictions about circuit behavior and could troubleshoot for opens and shorts to ground in series circuits. They went from getting all of the pre-test questions incorrect to getting all nine correct on the post-test (with the exception of one student who got two of the questions on the pre-test correct since he already had the basic concept of a circuit). The most impressive results were reflected in the students' troubleshooting behaviors. Several of the students modified the troubleshooting algorithm that the system demonstrated to make it more efficient. In other words, they understood circuit behavior and the trouble-shooting heuristics (such as divide the search space) well enough to make modifications. Another noteworthy aspect of the students' troubleshooting performances was that, when they made erroneous inferences, they were usually able to recover. For instance, they would reach a contradiction and recognize that one of the inferences they had made earlier was premature. Finally, on the post-test, students were given a troubleshooting problem of a type they had not seen before (involving the possibility that the fault could be either a short or an open), and all of the students were able to get the correct answer.

In their use of the system, all of the students were remarkably conservative. Typically, they did a large proportion of the problems in a given set, even though, after the first few problems, they were getting them all correct. The reason they often gave was that they were afraid of missing a "tricky" problem near the end of the set—"something I don't understand might be lurking in there." They rarely skipped a topic within the progression, and went through the set of models in the linear order of the curriculum. They only occasionally experimented with a circuit by, for instance, flipping switches or disconnecting parts. Instead, they primarily employed the learning strategy of going to a new topic (as embedded in the next qualitative model in the progression), trying a problem, getting it wrong, asking for an explanation, and then solving the rest of the problems (usually correctly). Occasionally, when the new topic was particularly novel (e.g., troubleshooting for the first time), they would request a demonstration/explanation before attempting a problem.

There are numerous possible reasons why the students employed this "conservative" learning strategy. First, the fact that the system presented a curriculum to the students implied that its designers believed it was a good idea to progress through the models in a linear order. If, instead, students had been presented with a network of increasingly sophisticated models, they would have been forced to decide on their own path through the model space and problem sets, and their behavior might have been quite different. Second, the students' conception of how one learns, derived from their school environment, is primarily that of following a curriculum by hearing explanations and then doing problems. So the fact that they employed this learning strategy when using the instructional system may simply be an instantiation of their school model of learning. Finally, when interacting with the system, the students were being observed. This may have inhibited their exploratory behavior and increased their desire to "do the right thing," i.e., get correct answers to problems as quickly as possible. They thus relied on the explanations, rather than on discovering model transformations for themselves.

The implications of these results are that in our future research, we should explicitly teach and encourage alternative learning strategies. For instance, we could apply the model progression concept to students' mental models of their own learning processes. Using the flexibility of QUEST, students could start with a familiar learning strategy, i.e. learning from examples and explanations, gradually progress to learning via induction and feedback, and finally be introduced to exploration and discovery learning. Through this progression, students could acquire these alternative learning strategies, as well as the skills needed for independent scientific inquiry.

5. Summary

The design of our intelligent learning environment is based upon a theory of expertise and its acquisition. We have argued that when reasoning about physical systems, experts utilize a set of mental models. For instance, they may use qualitative as well as quantitative models, and behavioral as well as functional models. The transition from novice to expert status can be regarded as a process of model evolution: students formulate a series of upwardly compatible models, each of which is adequate for solving some subset of problems within the domain. Further, students need to evolve, not just a single model, but rather a set of models that embody alternative conceptualizations of the domain. Finally, we claim that in the initial stages of learning, students should focus on the acquisition of qualitative, causal models. Algebraic, constraint-based reasoning should be introduced only after the domain is understood in causal terms.

In the article, we focused primarily on qualitative, behavioral models of electrical circuit operation which have been designed to make the causality of circuit behavior derivable, in a clearcut manner, from basic physical principles.

The constraints on model evolution, in terms of causal consistency, modifiability, and learnability, were discussed and a sequence of models that embody a possible transformation from novice to expert status was outlined.

The learning environment we have constructed lets students solve problems, hear explanations, and perform experiments, all in the context of interacting with a dynamic simulation of circuit behavior. However, unlike most simulations, the underlying model is qualitative not quantitative. Further, the simulation is performed not by a single model, but rather by a progression of causal models that increase in sophistication in concordance with the evolution of the students' understanding of the domain.

Viewing instruction as producing in the student a progression of models permits a tutoring system architecture with elegant properties. Within our system, the student model, the tutor, and the domain simulation are incorporated within the single model that is active at any point in learning. This model is used to simulate the domain phenomena, is capable of generating explanations by articulating its behavior, and furnishes a model of the students' reasoning at that particular stage in learning. The progression of models also enables the system to select problems and generate explanations that are appropriate for the student at any point in the instructional sequence. In order to motivate students to transform their models into new models, they are given problems that the new model can handle but their present model cannot. This evolution of models also enables the system to focus its explanations on the difference between the present model and the new model.

Such a system architecture also permits a variety of pedagogical strategies to be explored within a single instructional system. Since the system can turn a problem into an example by solving it for the student, the students' learning can be motivated by problems or by examples. That is, students can be presented with problems and only see examples if they run into difficulty; alternatively, they can see examples first and then be given problems to solve. Also, by working within the simulation environment, students can use a circuit editor to construct their own problems and thus explore the domain in a more open-ended fashion. The system is capable of generating runnable qualitative models for any circuit that the student or instructional designer might create. Further, the learning process can be directed either by the system or by the student. Students are provided with a map of the problem space, and can decide for themselves what class of problems to pursue next or even what pedagogical strategy they want to employ. Thus students can be actively engaged not only in problem solving but also in managing their learning.

ACKNOWLEDGMENT

This research was funded by the Army Research Institute, under contract MDA-903-87-C-0545, and by the Office of Naval Research and the Army Research Institute, under ONR contract N00014-82-C-0580 with the Personnel and Training Research Program. We are grateful to Judith

Oransanu of ARI, as well as to Marshall Farr and Susan Chipman of ONR for supporting and encouraging this work. The initial system prototype was programmed by Frank Ritter, who helped with its design, particularly the circuit orientation scheme and the user interface. The current implementation was programmed by Eric Cooper. We wish to thank Bill Clancey and two anonymous reviewers for their constructive comments on this paper. In addition, we are grateful to Allan Collins, Wally Feurzeig, Paul Horwitz, Ed Smith, Kathy Speohr, and Mark Burstein for many stimulating and helpful discussions.

REFERENCES

1. Anderson, J.R., Farrell, R. and Sauers, R., Learning to program in LISP, *Cognitive Sci.* **8** (1984) 87–129.
2. Bobrow, D.G. (Ed.), *Qualitative Reasoning about Physical Systems* (MIT Press, Cambridge, MA, 1985); also *Artificial Intelligence* **24** (1984) Special Volume.
3. Brown J.S. and Burton, R.R., Diagnostic models for procedural bugs in basic mathematical skills, *Cognitive Sci.* **2** (1978) 155–192.
4. Brown, J.S., Burton, R.R. and de Kleer, J., Pedagogical, natural language and knowledge engineering techniques in SOPHIE I, II and III, in: D. Sleeman and J.S. Brown (Eds.), *Intelligent Tutoring Systems* (Academic Press, New York, 1982).
5. Brown, J.S. and VanLehn, K., Repair theory: A generative theory of bugs in procedural skills, *Cognitive Sci.* **4** (1980) 379–426.
6. Bruner, J.S., Goodnow, J.J. and Austin, G.A., *A Study of Thinking* (Wiley, New York, 1956).
7. Chi, M., Feltovich, P. and Glaser, R., Categorization and representation of physics problems by experts and novices, *Cognitive Sci.* **5** (1981) 121–152.
8. Clancey, W.J., Qualitative student models, *Ann. Rev. Comput. Sci.* **1** (1986) 381–450.
9. Cohen, R., Eylon, B. and Ganiel, U., Potential difference and current in simple electric circuits: A study of students' concepts, *Am. J. Phys.* **51** (1983) 407–412.
10. Collins, A., Component models of physical systems, in: *Proceedings Seventh Annual Conference of the Cognitive Science Society*, Irvine, CA (1985).
11. Cronbach, L.J. and Snow, R.E., *Aptitudes and Instructional Methods: A Handbook for Research on Interactions* (Irvington, New York, 1977).
12. Davis, R., Reasoning from first principles in electronic troubleshooting, *Int. J. Man-Mach. Stud.* **19** (1983) 403–423.
13. de Kleer, J., Causal and teleological reasoning in circuit recognition, TR-529, MIT Artificial Intelligence Laboratory, Cambridge, MA (1979).
14. de Kleer, J., How circuits work, *Artificial Intelligence* **24** (1984) 205–280.
15. de Kleer, J. and Brown, J.S., Assumptions and ambiguities in mechanistic mental models, in: D. Gentner and A. Stevens (Eds.), *Mental Models* (Erlbaum, Hillsdale, NJ, 1983).
16. de Kleer, J. and Brown, J.S., A qualitative physics based upon confluences, *Artificial Intelligence* **24** (1984) 7–83.
17. di Sessa, A., Phenomenology and the evolution of intuition, in: D. Gentner and A. Stevens (Eds.), *Mental Models* (Erlbaum, Hillsdale, NJ, 1983).
18. Feltovich, P.J., Spiro, R.J. and Coulson, R.L., The nature of conceptual understanding in biomedicine: The deep structure of complex ideas and the development of misconceptions, in: D. Evans and V. Patel (Eds.), *The Cognitive Sciences in Medicine* (MIT Press, Cambridge, MA, 1989).
19. Feurzeig, W. and Ritter, F., Understanding reflective problem solving, in: J. Psotka, L.D. Massey and S. Mutter (Eds.), *Intelligent Tutoring Systems: Lessons Learned* (Erlbaum, Hillsdale, NJ, 1989).

20. Feurzeig, W. and White, B.Y., Development of an articulate instructional system for teaching arithmetic procedures, BBN Rept. No. 5484, BBN Laboratories, Cambridge, MA (1983).
21. Forbus, K.D., Qualitative process theory, *Artificial Intelligence* **24** (1984) 85–168.
22. Forbus, K. and Gentner, D., Causal reasoning about quantities, in: *Proceedings Eighth Annual Conference of the Cognitive Science Society*, Amherst, MA (1986).
23. Forbus, K. and Stevens, A.S., Using qualitative simulation to generate explanations. BBN Rept. No. 4490, BBN Laboratories, Cambridge, MA (1981).
24. Frederiksen, J. and White, B., Mental models and understanding: A problem for science education, in: *Proceedings NATO Advanced Research Workshop on New Directions in Educational Technology*, Milton Keynes, England (1988).
25. Frederiksen, J., White, B., Collins, A. and Eggan, G., Intelligent tutoring systems for electronic troubleshooting, in: J. Psotka, D. Massey and S. Mutter (Eds.), *Intelligent Tutoring Systems: Lessons Learned* (Erlbaum, Hillsdale, NJ, 1989).
26. Frederiksen, J. and White, B., Intelligent tutors as intelligent testers, in: N. Frederiksen, R. Glaser, A. Lesgold and M. Shafto (Eds.), *Diagnostic Monitoring of Skill and Knowledge Acquisition* (Erlbaum, Hillsdale, NJ, 1989).
27. Gentner, D. and Stevens, A.L., *Mental Models* (Erlbaum, Hillsdale, NJ 1983).
28. Goldstein, I.P., The genetic graph: A representation for the evolution of procedural knowledge, in: D. Sleeman and J.S. Brown (Eds.), *Intelligent Tutoring Systems* (Academic Press, New York, 1982).
29. Haertel, H., A qualitative approach to electricity, Rept. No. IRL87-0001, Xerox PARC, Palo Alto, CA (1987).
30. Horowitz, P. and Hill, W., *The Art of Electronics* (Cambridge University Press, Cambridge, 1980).
31. Kieras, D. and Bovair, S., The role of a mental model in learning to operate a device, *Cognitive Sci.* **8** (1984) 255–273.
32. Kuipers, B., Commonsense reasoning about causality: Deriving behavior from structure, *Artificial Intelligence* **24** (1984) 169–203.
33. Larkin, J.H., McDermott, J., Simon, D.P. and Simon, H.A., Expert and novice performance in solving physics problems, *Science* **208** (1980) 1335–1342.
34. Reiser, B.J., Anderson, J.R. and Farrell, R.G., Dynamic student modelling in an intelligent tutor for LISP programming, in: *Proceedings IJCAI-85*, Los Angeles, CA (1985) 8–14.
35. Richer, M.H. and Clancey, W.J., Guidon-Watch: A graphic interface for viewing a knowledge-based system, Department of Computer Science Rept. No. STAN-CS-85-1068, Stanford University, CA (1985).
36. Ritter, F., OREO: Adding orientation to a dynamic qualitative simulation, Rept. No. 6560, BBN Laboratories, Cambridge, MA (1987).
37. Rouse, W.B. and Morris, N.M., On looking into the black box: Prospects and limits in the search for mental models, Center for Man-Machine Systems Research Rept. No. 85-2, Georgia Institute of Technology, Atlanta, GA (1985).
38. Smith, E.E. and Goodman, L., Understanding instructions: The role of an explanatory schema, *Cognition and Instruction* **1** (1984) 359–396.
39. Sleeman, D. and Brown, J.S. (Eds.), *Intelligent Tutoring Systems* (Academic Press, New York, 1982).
40. Soloway, E., Learning to program = learning to construct mechanisms and explanations, *Commun. ACM* **29** (1986) 850–858.
41. Soloway, E., Rubin, E., Woolf, B., Bonar, J. and Johnson, W.L., Meno-II: An AI-based programming tutor, *J. Comput-Based Instruction* **10** (1983) 1.
42. Steinberg, M.S., Reinventing electricity, in: *Proceedings International Seminar, Misconceptions in Science and Mathematics*, Ithaca, NY (1983).
43. Weld, D., Explaining complex engineering devices, BBN Rept. No. 5489, BBN Laboratories, Cambridge, MA (1983).

44. Weld, D., The use of aggregation in causal simulation, *Artificial Intelligence* **30** (1986) 1–34.
45. White, B.Y. and Frederiksen, J.R., Modeling expertise in troubleshooting and reasoning about simple electric circuits, in: *Proceedings Annual Meeting of the Cognitive Science Society*, Boulder, CO (1984).
46. White, B.Y. and Frederiksen, J.R., QUEST: Qualitative understanding of electrical system troubleshooting, *ACM SIGART Newslett.* **93** (1985) 34–37.
47. White, B. and Frederiksen, J., Progressions of qualitative models as a foundation for intelligent learning environments, Rept. No. 6277, BBN Laboratories, Cambridge, MA (1986).
48. White, B. and Frederiksen, J., Intelligent tutoring systems based upon qualitative model evolutions, in: *Proceedings AAAI-86*, Philadelphia, PA (1986).
49. White, B. and Frederiksen, J., Qualitative models and intelligent learning environments, in: R. Lawler and M. Yazdani (Eds.), *AI and Education* (Ablex, New York, 1987).
50. White, B. and Horwitz, P., ThinkerTools: Enabling children to understand physical laws, Rept. No. 6470, BBN Laboratories, Cambridge, MA (1987).
51. Williams, B.C., Qualitative analysis of MOS circuits, *Artificial Intelligence* **24** (1984) 281–346.

Received March 1986; revised version received November 1987

Index